Let's Keep This Adventure Rolling

The Ride Continues, but the Worst Is Over!

Adventure 2

Jennifer

Sept. 2021

Jennifer Collins-Timm

PAGE PUBLISHING, INC.
Conneaut Lake, PA

First originally published by Page Publishing 2021

ISBN 978-1-6624-3678-9 (pbk)
ISBN 978-1-6624-3679-6 (digital)

Printed in the United States of America

To my Timm men, what an adventure we had created together—our little slice of Timm paradise! To my parents, for setting the example of how to go after our dreams with a little sweat, tears, and humor!

Adventure 2

Did you really think the ride ended with my first book *It's Been One Hell of a Ride*? Heck no! I must tell you all about our adventure and then the side journey that pushed its way in with this two-part book. *Let's Keep This Adventure Rolling* is our actual story on how we dealt with the desire to create a space where we could feel as if we were on vacation from the moment we pulled into our driveway. This is a story about coming together as a family to create a bit of paradise from all the things we had noticed that gave us a sense of peace or that made us scream, "This is so us!" and put gleaming smiles on our faces.

We are all called and pulled in different directions; it's up to us to figure out what we want, what draws our attention, and what gives us a feeling of our ultimate paradise. I do hope by sharing our story, you find Zen time in your own adventure. Let's do this together. Let's get this adventure rolling.

The Itch

Work hard—play hard and
don't worry about getting
a little dirt under your nails;
the lessons learned
during the process are well worth it!
—Collins' motto

One of the earliest memories I have is sitting in a grade-school classroom redesigning the room in my head—adding a couch here and a table there, debating with myself over a table lamp versus a floor lamp, painting the walls, determining a satin or semigloss paint finish and hanging some artwork, pondering apron-length soft curtains or sleek blinds. I had no idea what the teacher was talking about the majority of the time, nor did I even care; my mission was to figure out if a rectangle or an oval rug would look best in this space before the recess bell, and the pressure was on! Most likely, this is how I learned my shapes and vertical versus horizontal directions, not a classroom but in real-life applications in my chaotic head.

I feel I got this distracted obsession from my mother and her appointed duties as a contractor's wife. My hard-working father owned a home construction business, Collins Construction, in a small rural town in northwestern Iowa. It was a good, honest business and kept my dad working long, sawdust sweaty hours with his demanding and at-the-mercy-of-the-weather schedule.

Every five years, when my mom's Home Design folder was full, we either remodeled an extremely old home or built fresh from the ground up and moved in. Each home was drastically different inside and out. It was where they met with clients to discuss their own dream home desires. It was part of his business and part of our journey in my youth. My mom's mission was to make each of our own homes different from the last, and each home highlighted a supercool feature for its time—torch-burned rustic beams on a living room's ceiling, a master's bedroom with cowboy-swinging doors to the walk-in closet and bathroom. My older brother's bedroom separated by a firepole to his basement playroom. There was a front door to the mailbox path accented with an arched wooden walk bridge, a rather large sitting room with dark-wood-paneled walls, oriental rugs, and a dazzling chandelier, a kitchen stove showcased with an overhead brick arch, and a bedroom with a massive wall-size mirror and ballet bar. The things she came up with for each home created a space to be super proud of and ready to be shown to potential clients and, well, our friends.

The last home I lived in before heading off to college was a hundred-year-plus-old farmhouse a mile and a half outside of our petite farming town with a crumbling barn, rotting chicken coop, and many acres of timber that needed an insane overhaul—or a flick of a match and burn that monster to the ground because you are freaking kidding me if we are leaving a brand-new dream home in the heart of town and walking distance to all our friends for this horror story! Are you reading that as an emotional teenage girl screeching at her parents with tears and stomping feet? Yes, I may have been a bit dramatic as a teenager. But even my older brother's young wife let out a deep gasp, held hands to her chest with her eyes glazed over in disgust as we pulled up to this beast of a house for the first time. I couldn't have agreed with her more! It was to be our home to live in while the remodel took place, all while my younger sister, only by fourteen months, and I were in our high school years. Oh, the embarrassment! I mean really, we had to use a bathtub to wash our dishes the first whole summer while our kitchen was being built—what the hell! This chore sucked the big one as pampered teenagers coming from a brand-new showcase home with an actual working dishwasher—how could they do this to us?

To add to the dramatics of this nightmare we found ourselves in, my sister and I each had to gut our own rooms in order to even have a place to call a bedroom before winter arrived. And winter was coming, so a deadline was in place for us. Yes, you read that right; as sassy and maybe a tad spoiled teenage girls, we had to take a crowbar and hammer to break down layers of wallpaper, plaster, and lath to haul to the next room over then toss it all out the window to the dumpster below. This task needed to be performed in order to get to the bare studs of the wall so we could add up-to-code proper insulation before installing fresh dry-wall. This was quite the swearing, crying, screaming, some giggling, coughing dirt and dust farmer blowing into our shirts process. It was summer, hot and sticky. Even typing this almost twenty-seven-ish years later brings back memories of the stale, nasty dust in the air. The layers of filth on us and the gruesomeness we were pulling from those hundred-year-plus walls—walnuts, glass jars, snake skins, newspapers, dead bees, what the hell is that, you name it, it was in those walls.

At the time, it was absolutely blistering, exhausting work for teenagers who would rather be out cruising in the summer sun with our friends. But we soon realized what a rewarding experience it was because we were part of the decorating and personalizing details—paint, carpet, and bedding, we had input on it all, with Mom's approval, of course. My sport-oriented sister went for the Americana look with soft baby-blue walls and carpet. An Americana quilt and matching throw pillows were ordered. The finishing touches included her assorted horse figurines on wooden shelves. I—being a tad umm, well, just me—desired a completely opposite atmosphere. Mom understood me and was so cool to be up on the latest sponge painting craze; therefore, extremely dark-navy walls with splashes of soft lavender and metallic gold were tried and perfected! Very dark navy plush carpet was laid. My room was topped off with a lava lamp, a wall covered with quirky velvet hats, and a beaded curtain to my closet. My super crafty mom even took it to the next level and sewed a patchwork quilt with colorful laces and velvets to polish off the look. I was so darn in awe of this room. The whole room screamed to me at the time. And right there is where I got *the itch* that rolled with me into my adult years.

Now going back to this hundred-year-plus-old farmhouse, which I couldn't wait to get away from to start my own adventure, is a true testament of what a little sweat, cussing, a great vision, and hard work can achieve. The crumbling barn was soon replaced by a three-car garage plus a bonus heated shop with a wall-to-wall countertop that's perfect for a large get-together. The rotted chicken coop is now sporting a brand-new super-sized metal building that use to store all Dad's construction equipment before his retirement. The land around the house covered with multiple gardens that any master gardener would dream about, and the garden tours my mother puts on are a hit. The far lot has the most amazing tree house with gazebo, bridge, double-hammock hut, and firepole for all the grandkids to spend hours giggling on. This treehouse was honestly built for my mom to play on and have a fantasy reading spot but watching her grandkids play on it, put the cherry on top. More surrounding acres were purchased for hunting, and ponds were constructed to host fishing, swimming, and grilling at family gatherings. The house was lifted to have a full-finished basement for Dad to hideout in and store Mom's garden seeds for the winter. A reading room was added, with wall-to-wall windows to watch the wildlife from the indoor hammock. They included a three-season room off the back of the house with a hot tub for night soaking of their achy, aging bodies. They had a vision and went after it. It may had taken years to create the perfect play and relaxation space, but really, is any space complete as we grow and change?

Our homes should reflect our life vision boards, not what is *in* at the time according to corporate advertisements and not what your neighbor has or what would impress others but what speaks to you and what can grow with you. It should be a space where you can get creative with and try new things. Create a home that tells your story and fill it with objects, colors, and textures that bring a smile to your face and that are parts of your adventure. Plus the ultimate lesson: partaking in a home remodel is not going to kill you but more likely mold a more responsible, multitasking, hardworking, and creative adult.

There's a Process to My Madness

Don't change so people will like
you. Be yourself and the right
people will love the real you.
—Unknown

From my first apartment to home after home after home with my man on my arms, I was decorating, redecorating, and wandering for hours around home improvement stores for ideas. These were the days way before spending insomnia hours on Pinterest and making idea folders on a computer. This saint of a man I've been blessed with got my full obsession to details during a shopping trip for our first apartment's shower curtain together. The poor thing thought this was a "run to the nearest store, grab the first shower curtain package on shelf and call it good." Oh, sweet baby Jesus, was he in for a surprise how this gal processes, dissects, and changes her mind! Because hold on tight, dear, we will be running all over the state—quite possibly the Midwest—to look at every store to see what they have to offer. Therefore, this may take a month or two, but I am determined we will find *that* shower curtain that speaks to me! I see it in my head, so it must be out there. A strange quirk since I am not a shopper at all—well, not for clothing anyway—but I do enjoy browsing for hours through a home improvement store or three! And seeing that 11 percent rebate sign... Oh, boy!

The first house my man and I bought together in our very early twenties was a small original-wood floor, three-bedroom, one-bathroom, with ivory siding and navy-blue shutter seventies style ranch with a single car attached garage. I couldn't wait to get in it to add my... I mean, umm, *our* (with my approval) personal touch. Those were the days when wallpapers and borders were the latest and greatest every home must have, so *they* said. Hand slap to the forehead, what were we all thinking! Still wondering who *they* were. In this house, I felt like every room needed to have its own theme or personality, so of course, I put our experienced folks to work right away hanging wallpaper in the cove-ceiling living room. I envisioned classy and fancy with a pattern of tan, narrow colonial vertical columns wrapped with floral leaves in hints of burgundy, navy, and hunter green on every single flipping wall. It was, what would the kids say today for "on point"—sick? epic? gnarly? (I'm trying here, I have no idea what the hell kids are saying these days. I'm tired and numb, and my hearing is on low charge.) It was the perfect backdrop for my oversized light-oak china hutch sporting our numerous collections of wedding crystal that I just had to have at the time. This is now a "what was I thinking?" moment looking back. I was trying to play a part of a mature, have it all together, nice wife, and apparently, crystal and wallpaper screamed it at the time. Thank you, my saint of a mother, for taking all those pieces off my hands when I came back to reality many years later. They are fabulously stored away safely in her own hutch. It's simply amazing how those dainty pieces made it through a few homes untouched by my spirited, young Timm boys whom I was so blessed with. They must have sensed JennJenn would unleash the dragon if they even glanced in their shiny, delicate direction. Good boys, you always did listen after encouraging a few full-blown freak-outs and meltdown performances from me—we rocked the dramatic scenes well together and deserved an Oscar; take a bow with me, my boys.

The dreamiest tiny nursery was designed in this ranch home, knowing we were having a boy because this gal is not a fan of surprises and I had decorating to do. A busy, busy bee I was. The walls were painted a soft periwinkle. Yeah, that's a fun name to say, but it was sky blue; sky blue was the real color. Anyhoo, the sky blue–periwinkle walls were then sponge painted white and stenciled with bright-yellow stars. Even glow-in-the-dark stars in a variety of sizes were added to the ceiling, yet another room covered from floor to ceiling, wall to wall. Go big or go home seems to be our life theme! The Noah's Ark–quilted bedding set, wall hangings, and matching curtains were bought and displayed without a wrinkle to be seen. Ryan and I stood back to admire with the Happy Chef proud smile. It was adorable, makes me smile with pride still. My excited mom, a soon-to-be three-time grandma, showed off the picture of the room to all her friends, leaving with the comment from one: "They are

Yuppies, huh?" Not sure if that was good or bad, but I'll take it—proud Yuppies, we were! This room was rarely actually slept in by our first Timm boy, Ethan, but frequently witnessed his colic episodes in it. Maybe he was trying to tell us something? Jeez, JennJenn, he wanted balls, balls, and balls, not calming, dreamy stars, and periwinkle, really? But our content Evan got plenty of long z's in it!

After a few years of enjoying our first adorable home, which was obnoxiously covered in wallpaper, bold primary colors, and accent borders, we placed a sold sign in the front yard and packed up our two young Timm boys to make a quick move to a rental townhome in a northern neighboring community with a new career for my Ryan. Quite possibly, it was a break from home ownership constant projects for him as well. Happy to give you a vacay, dear, for now. This new community and the rental were short-lived. I feel because he was freaked out a stranger was sleeping on the other side of the thin wall from him. But he would say a home was calling our name near his folks in yet another neighboring A-named community to settle long-term and raise our Timm boys through their school years. Ryan quickly checked it out and bought it onsite without me even seeing it. *Surprise!* There is no messing around with this man. But he knew I would love it and would get busy with plans for it either way. By this time, he was firm with "whatever, just hire it done" as he gently waved for me to step aside from the big screen. Good man, I've trained you well.

In the early years of homeownership, being employed as an in-home decorating consultant had its benefits, according to me. I'm sure quite the headache with an eye roll for my "just keep it simple" man—a large TV with remote, comfy chair, and a small refrigerator end table with bare white walls are all that is needed in a home. Thank God he had me to fix this insanity! I had the pleasure to see a wide assortment of homes and décor every single day. Plus, I was surrounded with dazzling home décor advertisements in this profession, which got me spinning with ideas to tackle in our own home, then adding the mix of my upbringing of remodeling and living in "ready to show at any time" homes. Although, in all honesty, it created a monster for this type-A personality gal, and I regularly obsessed over making everything picture-perfect. I'm so sorry, Timm men! JennJenn, just breathe and repeat: not all needs to be perfect to be perfect. But let me clarify one thing: toilet paper needs to roll from the top to be perfect—don't screw that up! I even once told my family at a very young age that Mom and Dad couldn't live with me when they were old because they would be shaky, and I would have very nice, fragile things. Ha! At least I was honest; I knew what I desired and made it perfectly clear so they all could get a future plan in place for them without including me.

Now this "surprise" split-level home introduced us to our first encounter of an overly friendly, knowing-our-entire-business neighbor. In our apartment, first home, and townhome rental, we knew our neighbors by sight—a gentle nod, friendly smile, a wave, and into our safe houses we all went, but this was a whole new introduction to *neighborhood watch*, apparently. We totally missed that memo. We're friendly, and we truly enjoy your time, but we desire and thoroughly cherish our own private, quiet space after a wild, demanding day out in the human world.

After knocking out some upper divider kitchen cabinets and putting a fresh coat of the perfect shade of bold red on the walls, the next surface was screaming for a makeover. While a contractor was busy working his skills installing the new countertops, I get a call on my cell phone while away at the office, the voice in full enthusiasm, "I love your new countertops!"

Awkward pause and silence, I'm so confused... "Say what?" Holy moist, supersized porcupine balls! (Do you like that word, *moist*? My sister sure does. I added it in for full dramatics of the scene we were living at the time.) Oh boy, how am I going to explain this one to my Ryan that the friendly neighbor is sitting in our home, on his couch, *watching* the new countertops being installed with her kiddos! The "door is always open" has begun and felt so freaking weird. Neighborhood watch party has now been taken to the next level, and I don't remember signing up for this service.

Two-ish years at this multi-split-level home with every surface rocking a new top-notch look, we needed to breathe and spread out a bit more. I mean really, Timm boys (or should I say Timm men), this was our second home together with only *one* bathroom! I'm a trooper, but enough is enough. JennJenn needs a toilet seat to place her buns without pee on it! Therefore, a brand-spanking-new large home was purchased in an upcoming neighborhood a few blocks over, a home I would normally target as a client in my in-home decorating consultant days. My head was ready to explode at the possibilities to do with this beast! The door had been opened wide for Mr. Insomnia to step in—"Welcome" with a grand, elegant curtesy.

This story and a half-light oak here, there, and every-where—you know what I'm talking about, the light oak craze and *everyone* who was anyone had it. Our Ethan would say, "Everyone is doing it. Everyone has it. Everyone, everyone…" As I'm typing this, about a dozen of you are sanding, priming, and painting this light oak white, right? You were caught up in the madness too; I get it. This home was purchased in the building stage. Therefore, we had the pleasure to pick out all the finishing touches. Floor tile, carpet, lighting fixtures, and countertops, oh my, were con-firmed in a breeze—imagine that! You name it, we got to pick it, and we continued the finishing touches the ten-plus years we lived there.

Being a project gal, the space was never finished-fin-ished as new ideas, plans, and interests were always exposed to us—or me. I didn't know any better; this was how I was raised, so I continued the pattern of "keep updating, keep changing out the look." I even let the boys add their own touches in their bedrooms. We hired an artist to come in to paint massive silhouettes of skateboarders on a wall over a bed; that later brought on nightmares. Well, that was a bust—hand slap to the forehead, shaking my head. Another bedroom was requested with a different primary color on each wall, so it looked like a Crayola box threw up, and sensory overload was achieved.

As Ryan studied sports stats, I studied paint chips. I mean, really, the season had changed, so a room called for a new color, making the room square footage once again a millimeter smaller with each layer. Many girls changed out purses, shoes, and their entire closet with each season; I'll admit it, I'm just not that type of gal. I even went so far as to owning my own paint chip color wheel from the local paint store, as their staff became my BFFs, because I needed to see the colors in every lighting—morning, noon, and night. Sunny days and rainy days, even my mood from day to day determined which shade we were going to go with. All while my Ryan stood behind me saying through the years, "Can't we just have white walls?" Silly man, that is so boring (then). Besides, there are over fifty shades of white. Shall we start the process of determining if we want a pink-white, blue-white, yellow-white, dirty white etc.? No? Let's just stick with some color and even more color on accented walls, okay? Okay. Now one thing I didn't press on was, he *did. not. paint*, period. So, I made sure not to cross the line there. "But, honey, can you run to the store to get me two gallons of this and that?" was always achieved with a kiss and flutter of my eyes.

We craved to be outside and made our backyard our own little slice of paradise, our outdoor living room to escape to after long, stressful days in the office or after an evening of running those Timm boys and a handful of their friends. The patio was framed with trees, bushes, and flowers of every texture and color to enjoy with a drink or four and just chill to get ready for the next marathon day. Ryan desired a pool to be shoved in this little lot, but I just couldn't see us relaxing in it as we were already exposed to the world being a corner lot backed up to another home—Well, hello, Timms, what do we have here, can we join you?

Hold on tight, secure your seatbelts, grab anything you can, we're going to make a sharp turn with tires squealing very soon on this adventure! We spent ten-plus years in that quarter-acre corner lot, story and a half, home. It was a glorious drop-grab-and-go grand home during our crazy schedules with these wild Timm boys. I accommodated the males with their own game room, a theater room, and one-and-half-story mini basketball court in our main living room. Accommodated? Or maybe ignored what they created, so I could use that male bonding time doing my own thing. I totally enjoyed my own bathroom with no pee on the seat too—winning! But we were entering the mid-teen years with these boys and a used car lot look with late hours coming and going was soon to be part of the Timm party. Plus, we just didn't need to add more tension to the neighborhood gang—roll of the eyes and a teasing wink.

It was time for a change, time for a new scenery, and time to move on. I was utterly heartbroken over a loss of our buddy, pal, and love, my baby, Ed the boxer. We were caught up in yet another Ethan health hiccup (stay tuned, you will get the full gossip soon enough; just be a tad more patient, my dear). Our careers were both demanding. I was beyond annoyed with the constant annoyances of neighborhood living and was honestly feeling the urge to tell everyone to *fuck off* while going through my grief. Hey, I said I was being honest, possibly needed more naps during those days. I wished I knew about CBD oil and, for sure, should have had less wine. Oh well, what's done is done.

Life goes on. I was so over it, trying to keep up cleaning the supersized home with rooms we didn't even use but were decorated up with unnecessary furniture to dust. As read in my first book *It's Been One Hell of a Ride*, we said no more excuses and went out on a whim and bought ourselves a much-dreamed-about acreage. Without even officially advertising and in only one and a half days, we received an offer on our beast of a house while sitting in a surgery center waiting room for our Ethan—*booyah!* We are rolling on to a new adventure. And boy, were we giddy!

Too many times, people just settle for what is and make do with their situation. But there are so many opportunities available to us; take a deep breath and look around. We all have dreams but seem too scared to act on them. The time may not seem right; the schedules are too full to add anything more, and what would people think? But you will kick yourself if you don't chase after something you always have in your thoughts and just can't shake off. Remember, we only get one chance at this ride—*one*. When you are at wit's in, just do it and take the leap. It's time for a change. It's a scary step and may feel a bit chaotic in the midst of it, but trust me, it always works out for the best in the end. Go after that wild adventure you have been seeing in your dreams, screaming yeehaw the whole way!

The Crack House

Home is Home…be it ever so humble…
—My wise, patient Ryan

Pulling onto this gravel driveway of a three-acre property on the edge of town with the faded mint-green metal siding and pink stone fifties-style ranch home for the first time had my man in an awkward silence, but open-minded. The realtor we knew through professional settings was a bit stunned, or should I say embarrassed as he stood outside, quite possibly pondering what the hell are these crazy Timms thinking while exploring the interior of this "quarter the size of what they currently have" home.

Walking in from the rear petite porch, we were greeted with the lovely musty smell of a closed-up older home during the summer months. I instantly noted the U-shaped kitchen table booth with original tweed cobalt-blue fabric cushions that reminded me of my grandparents' camper back in my pigtail days. I glanced over the orange kitchen cabinets in all their glory. We turned sideways to squeeze by the refrigerator that jutted out into the walk space. I eyed the assortment of stained carpet in the kitchen, living room, creepy dark hallway, bedrooms, and even in the bathroom. Carpet in the bathroom? The horror. (Keep your cool, Jenn.) My hand glided over the pink-and-gray stone fireplace with a gold enclosure. I admired the layers of brass designer rods and sun-blocking, dusty custom drapery that I'm sure an in-home decorating consultant made a wonderful commission on back in the day. I noted the rotting wood-framed, single-pane windows in every room and the solid no-sun-welcoming glass exterior doors. I was digging the dark vertical paneling on a number of the walls. I silently smirked at the baby-blue corner tub with mint-green plastic tile in the tiny main bathroom. The variety of pastel floral wallpaper in several rooms didn't even faze me. Many ideas where running through my mind as I walked through the floor plan without a word. I looked at Ryan with excitement, a twinkle in my eyes, and I burst out, *"It's perfect!"* He smiled big, showing those Timm dimples, knowing if I said that, then it certainly would be perfect, even if he couldn't see it, not even a little bit. Oh, the possibilities that I saw didn't align to what he saw, but he saw it all wrong. This man…thank goodness he had me. I walked him through it again waving my ideas here and there, pointing out what would be removed, widened, and what would be added. I designed it beautifully in the air, calculating the game plan, replaying the to-do list, and it clicked for him then. With full enthusiasm, we marched outside and announced, *"We want it.* This is exactly what we are looking for!" Understandably, matched by the realtor's jaw-dropping, nervous laugh, and stunned eyes, let's hurry up and get this in writing before these obviously delirious Timms come to their senses!

Now remember, our story-and-a-half home was sold extremely fast, so a quick possession was frantically needed, and thankfully, the fifty-style ranch was vacant. Therefore, we were accommodated by the two realtors that had acquired it with their own vision to update and flip it. Ha, we get to have all the *fun*! Let's get this show on the road and the tornado of the plans out of my head!

This was all going down as our Evan was entering his freshman year and Ethan his junior year of high school. We were between the summer activities. I was home with Ethan while he recovered from a mysterious nasal/polyp surgery, and our volunteering days had come to a complete halt. And yet it all happened so fast that we realized, "Hmm, we hadn't told our family and friends." So in true Timm fashion, we did a one-time announcement on social media: "Oh did we tell you we bought an acreage and sold our house quickly. Since we're home with Big-E recovering we have time to sort and box up the house. We are just positive our boxer Ed is our angel above blessing this new adventure. We shall giggle and skip through the next few months, as we always do—yeehaw!"

Even though we got a quick possession, Ryan and I still found ourselves driving the two miles out to our new (old) home the weeks leading up to the big move to enjoy some cold ones in our "we can't wait to have" wide-open backyard with our folded sport bag chairs, nice and handy in our trunk. Not a human in sight, "Oh those are locust" singing to us in the trees and the wonderful view of corn fields, the chemical free lawn, skyline and tiny glimpse of houses in the far distance. We were thrilled that soon, we will have this peaceful feeling daily. Awe, we can breathe—let them breathe!

Anxiously, moving day had arrived. It was super easy since much of our furniture and belongings were not coming into the house during the remodel. The original game plan in our heads was to have a few months to do the remodel while living in the updated, clean house in town. *Curb check*! Plans changed, and we Timms were ready to roll with this one too. We piled our multiple rooms of furniture into the two-and-a-half car detached garage that use to be the old man's seed shop with more belongings and new purchases for the remodel into the single car attached garage. It was a maze of organized chaos and we made sure that the boys had everything needed for school and activities in their vehicles safe and sound.

Here we are, our Timm boys were into their high school years, and we left an updated supersized dream home in town near their friends—sounding familiar? Hmm, history is repeating itself. Jeez, JennJenn, how could you do this to your own offspring? Oh, the humility! But this ranch did have a dishwasher and actual insulated walls, so you have *nothing* to complain about cupcakes! The front living room was sporting the boys' mattresses directly on the floor in front of the large rotted picture window for the first few months of ownership so that we could get the basement and bedrooms tackled. We had absolutely nothing in those orange kitchen cabinets because we knew those were going right away, and well, you all know I'm not a kitchen kind of gal.

And now we are back to sharing *one* damn bathroom again because the basement bathroom was screaming for attention first. We immediately sat down as a family and made a list—a growing taped-together list of what must be tackled in each room. Let's get rolling with this game plan in place!

Among the organized chaos, Ethan being Ethan, kept his revolving door of entourage coming through the house with absolutely no shame as he announces, "Welcome to the Crack House!" with his arms wide open and gleaming, Timm dimple out, proud.

I feel the greatest lesson we learned from the moving adventure is that less really is more. Purging of material things and downsizing is a very freeing feeling! We didn't even miss or remember what we sold off, left, or donated. Obviously, it wasn't meaningful stuff, just money wasted stuff. A good purge every ten years is a must because really, "Where the hell did all this stuff come from, and why did we have it in the first place?" I challenge you all to walk around your own homes and do your own purge party. Keep it simple, folks. Remove the stuff from your view. Less is more!

The Stripping Party

If it doesn't add to your life, it
doesn't belong in your life
—Unknown

The moment the paperwork was signed, the property was officially ours, and the dumpster promptly arrived; it was game on! The dumpster gave us the green light; with crow bar and sledgehammer in hand, this mama was ready to release her crazy, which is normally fastened in a bit. Look out, Timm men, you've been warned! First thing's first, the layers of blinds, drapes, and valances must go. Dust, rods, and all, they were not welcomed to stay. We ran from room to room making sure not a single one was overlooked. Boom, just like that, the house looked brighter, and we were exposed to the beautiful vacant views!

Next up on the list, let's get the original 1950s hollow dark doors out of here. There were so many! Doors, doors, and more doors, like a crazy carnival house or a gameshow! What is my prize behind door number five? We only kept the bathroom door. Not sure why though, because for some reason, we don't seem to be a close-the-bathroom-door kind of family. We didn't touch the four basement room doors only because those were super stellar, custom-cedar planked doors. You just don't see those anymore. They remind me of a rustic cabin, so we were inspired to run with that look down below. We were thrilled with the freedom to open burn on the outskirts of town and had our burn pile glowing morning, noon, and night. The moment the Timm men threw those doors on the fire, they were ashes—a very scary thought, if ever a housefire.

The time had arrived to get that nasty carpet out! Oh, sweet baby Jesus was that disgusting with the years of dust, dirt, and not-sure-what-that-is foreign objects found under the carpet that would make anyone gag and want to take a shower in bleach. We started in the back rooms and worked our way out to the boys' camp-out front room. Cutting up into large squares, rolling up like a burrito, and hauling out to the majestic burn pile, sending smoke signals into town that the stripping party is in full swing and the Timms were having a blast! We crouched down like a camping buddy taking on a role of a fire God, with arms up, and demanded out loud, *"Fire!"*

Oh man, did that main floor tiny bathroom need us next. The baby-blue carpet got stripped in seconds. The mint-green plastic wall tile fell off with minimal effort from our Evan as he stood barefoot on the toilet seat with a scraper. I, on the opposite wall, was peeling off the wallpaper like it was an expired holiday curled up, static cling. It was begging to be removed and terribly tired of trying to hang on for dear life.

Next to focus on were those orange kitchen cabinets and upright hall cabinet taking up space in the kitchen.

Whoa, Nelly, it was time for those to go! They gave the men the most trouble. It appeared that the original builder, in the fifties, was concerned of a tornado taking them out; therefore, long spikes were used to drive them into the wall studs to stay in place until the end times. Never fear, we had power tools as back up to the sledgehammer, and the Timm men never give up without a good fight consisting of sweat, cussing, and a bit of blood. We are Timms; hear us roar. The first aid kit was nearby, and thankfully, a few licensed RNs were in the family too.

Now that this room was stripped, carpet and all, it was a glorious clean slate. My opportunity to turn it into whatever I would like when I visualized blaring the music, shaking my hips and singing, "Play that funky music, white boy!" Oh wait, stop. That's a different story. That was my dear mother after one beer many years ago, the first time introducing Ryan to my folks. It was her performance in the kitchen that Ryan walked in on that put a ring on my finger. Ryan was like, "Hell yeah, I want into this family!" Anyhoo, back to this blank space, we had to make this an awesome kitchen to blare our funky music in.

Ethan was coming and going—grabbing power tools and hauling out overgrown bushes, sweat pouring off his back, attaching chains to his SUV to show the stubborn roots who was the boss. It was no surprise; our quiet, go-with-the-flow Evan held down that floor mattress in the front room and snuggled in with our pug, Oliver. Quite content, this is no biggie. Lounge wear on with a bag of chips and a video handy, they were completely oblivious to the Timm show in progress around them. Evan embraced the vibe of the property from day one, way before the rest of us did. A time to relax, a camping and vacation feel without a concern in the world. Dudes, just sit back and chill. What's the rush?

While all this was going down, plumbing contractors were called in to tackle the bathroom toilets, vanities, and even the beautiful big baby-blue cast iron corner tub, big Bertha. The tub that we crouched down into with a hand-held shower nozzle for a good month as our only means of bathing ourselves. It brought us back to our camping days with a drizzle of water on us while exposed and cold to the world. Plumbers get paid well to touch nastiness, and for some reason, they actually show up to do this job when they say they will. While this company was full force into bathroom stripping, they discovered some piping issues, therefore, decided to take the party down to the concrete basement floor with jackhammers and came across the main pipe rotted out. Awesome. Can you hear the cha-ching as we grinned and shook our heads through this one? All new plumbing and fresh, new concrete flooring were added to the receipt pile. Kudos to those plumbers. They were the life of the party and got down and dirty—just how we like it! Plus, they cleaned up after themselves. They will continue to stay on our party list, and I told everyone to include on their list as well.

Now the house was mostly stripped for what we were planning to do ourselves as a family with our limited skills. Professionals were called in and presented us with at least one working industrial-looking bathroom with acid-stained concrete floors and sporting a super cool cedar upright shower before being called away to another larger ticket project with a more demanding deadline. We waited for their return and waited and waited some more. We learned even dangling a sizeable deposit check will have you waiting. Yep, we were stood up more times than we could count. Amazing how chillax we were about all of it. Don't get me wrong, we were anxious to continue the party, but we were still in the honeymoon stage of this adventure, so we took the excuses with patience. The boys continued on with their schedules without a care of the delays at home. One weeknight as the Timm boys were away at their activities, Ryan and I may have had a few drinks while reviewing the to-do list and got curious and a bit sassy, "How hard can taking down a wall actually be?" With a crowbar and sledgehammer in arm's reach, Ryan stood up, aimed, and threw in the first hit and looked over at me with a mischievous twinkle in his eyes paired with a wide grin. Oh, buddy, step aside; I want to give this a try too. What a flipping rush! We were releasing some tension we didn't realize we had. We giggled with every force hit into the plaster walls because baby, *we like demo*, as every blow left us evidence of our progress. A situation that should have had us totally stressed out was a freaking thrill to come home to tackle the day's aggression with humor every step of the way. Oh, look at that, we now have a hole in the bathroom wall open to the outside—now that wasn't on the to-do list.

We spent our weekdays in the office in daily washed clothes—to remove the demo dust—and our nights and weekends in dirty jeans, ripped shirts, with rags tied around our mouths and noses tearing down walls and widening openings. We snapped pictures and took videos to send to my busy, miles/hours-away construction dad for advice and guidance then dug in for some more. The only advice our licensed electrician had before leaving on a Friday evening was, "Just don't cut into any wires." So umm, yeah, in true Timm style, we did exactly that—cut right through a wire within an hour of his instructions. No biggie, no ER trips, no permed hair or smoke out of the nostrils. Maybe a spark or two and our hearts frozen in fright for a second. It's all good. Just gave Ryan a little jolt, and now we know his ticker can stop and start again smoothly. *"Hello, Mr. Insurance man, I would like to up that life insurance once again."* Many confirm drinking and driving is dangerous and should never be done. Let us Timms be the first to give the disclaimer, "Drinking and demoing should be banned as well." We seem to always be game to push an experience to the next level. We shall start a new support group called BUZZ: Bringing Unusual Zany Zest back into life of old homes and marriages! Who's game to join us?

> *"Ethan, for the love of God, stop inviting people into the house! We have no walls, no flooring, there are mattresses in random rooms, and a stove in the living room—no one needs to see our crazy, adventure up close!"*

We allowed the Timm boys to have some fun in our playhouse during the stripping party as well. I left notes on walls with Sharpies for anyone and everyone taking part to know what the plans were for that area. So the plumber,

HVAC guys, electrician, and my Timm men left drawings and comments too. We even let the bare subfloor sport some unusual artwork from our Evan—hand to the forehead and a great sigh. We just ran with it, and if anything seemed a bit questionable in nature, I just slapped some paint over it. No big penis and testicles artwork this time, so we were making progress there!

What we learned was, you can adjust to your chaos with humor and ease. While living in a house that is being remodeled, you still can get dressed up for work and nights out with friends. Just grab your clothes from the closet and give it a good shake or place outside on a windy day to remove demo dust, because tarps, plastic, and sheets won't stop that crap from settling—it just keeps coming! It's like sand at the beach or glitter in the craft room. Oh, and honey, control your excitement and don't install new, flipping cool light fixtures and ceiling fans until the demo project is complete—totally complete. Some dust just never ever comes out no matter how much scrubbing you apply. This is the biggest tip I could hand over to you from our adventure. Bonus tip: always listen very closely to your electrician's instructions. You are welcome.

The Worst Is Over

When you find people who not only
tolerate your quirks but celebrate
them with cries of "me too!" be
sure to cherish them, because
those weirdos are your tribe.

—A. J. Downey

During this new adventure, Ryan and I were fresh off from a vacay in Cape Cod, Massachusetts. Thank you to my new sister-in-law for introducing and welcoming us to her hometown—a fabulous, adorable town where they name their homes. On this trip, we walked around reading off and giggling over many of the names, and it inspired us to bring this amusement back home with us. In our camping days with our close friends, it was always joked those weekends were Zen time–Jenn time, a place for Mama to chill and relax. Therefore, we combined the naming idea with our young nephews' gesture of saying he's heading to the ranch because he had a two-story home, and his folks had to explain to him that our new (old) home was considered a ranch style since it was one level. Therefore, August 2014, The Zen Ranch was officially established. I envisioned a space to bring a sense of relaxation and calm, a cabin-cottage feel with an industrial-modern twist. There were so many times in life I could remember wanting to run away. We realized The Zen Ranch was where we wanted to run away to, our little slice of heaven where there is no need to dream of a vacation away. This was going to be our playhouse, our fun house, the perfect setting for our boys and all their friends' last years at home with us, a place they could come and go as loud as they wanted without disturbing any neighbors and could have bonfires all hours of the night.

The house remodel was so rewarding and exciting seeing it all come together with its unique character, bringing in all the feelings and interests that caught our attention from our own vacation stays yet working with the quirks of the fifties-style home. Evan announced, "It's like Christmas getting to pick out new things all the time." My Ryan found himself taking PTO days from the office to do some playing around the house and surprised the hell out of all of us by updating the dark, almost-black old paneling with rustic cedar planked walls framing a new white trimmed window. Our boys approved with full shock that their just hire-it-done dad had such skills hidden away. My sackin' fish has now earned another title: the greatest man a project gal could ever ask for, and boy, was my heart racing and head spinning with even more ideas to toss his way!

Let's just say remodeling a house is quite interesting with many lessons learned. The scheduling of various subcontractors in the correct order was a balancing act to stay on schedule—our constantly adjusted schedule. What once was anxiously frustrating with a few cuss words under the breath had turned into delirious humor and bets among the entire family, including numerous extra teenagers, who would show up as scheduled. The hired electricians, HVAC, and plumbers earn a high five, shout out, applause in my book. Every inch of The Zen Ranch was touched by these gentlemen, and I highly recommended them out on social media for their professionalism, knowledge, services, and prices—oh, and their patience with me. I may not have had kitchen cabinets, finished walls or flooring, but dang, check out my pipes, vents, and wires! It truly is the little things in life that make us do a happy dance.

> *Tested and proven; sawing, hammering, drilling, vacuuming, and pounding paint can lids on does not, I repeat, does not wake up teenage sleeping beauties! Heck, you can do all this, leave for the home improvement store, come back, grab the rest of your clan for an early dinner out, arrive back home to be surprised an extra teenager had appeared from their basement hibernation.*

Our first official holiday in The Zen Ranch, three quick months into the adventure, we still had exposed studded bare walls and unfinished ceilings in what needed to be a finished kitchen, said my man. The refrigerator had now joined the stove in our living room, one lonely new kitchen cabinet found its way into the front entry hallway, and we needed professional help on how to add a beam for the new widened entrances into this area. All the local contractors had no interest to step in on a fifties ranch home—little projects during the finally booming-again housing industry; therefore, construction gurus Mom and Dad came rolling into town for the rescue! We are forever grateful they spent their 2014 Thanksgiving Day with us getting down and dirty, sweat dripping; we're having fun now, coughing, sneezing, farmer blowing, and giggling. Dad was instructing my Ryan step by step with patience and humor, but before we knew it, he pushed him aside and was up on a step stool, power tools in hand with his bummed shoulder, cutting into our ceiling, cutting away wire mesh, and letting a waterfall of attic insulation artistically pile onto the kitchen (the room hasn't honestly earned this title as of yet though) floor, all while Mom and I were nearby as the assistants and clean-up crew questioning if that was really necessary. Men! Dad was in his element, giddy grin on, and Ryan was fired up to be his apprentice, taking it all in and glancing around to where else they could do some damage, as Dad kept reassuring us, "The worst is over." When there's a mess to be made, Dad is all about jumping in, and boy, do Ryan and I know how to give our guests the full experience and send them home with battle wounds to show they had an epic time.

Seeing my man's skills from the front-room cedar-planked walls and his apprenticeship knowledge got me waving him over to add whitewashed planked walls behind the freshly delivered stainless-steel refrigerator and stove. Ethan jumped in with full enthusiasm that he was now Dad's apprentice for the job because there were power tools involved! (Yes, and that fully stocked first aid kit still nearby.) I sat back taking in the scene and reminiscing to the days back in our very first home, that tiny ranch. Our Ethan and all his baby chubbiness as a toddler would put his boots on with his summer shorts (a look passed down from his great-grandpa Dave), his work goggles on upside down, and Ryan's winter head band on to hold back any sweat, he grabbed his "shoeshriver" and his "hhaa-mmer" to work on the house because it was broken. This whole view many years later stilled my heart to the quieter, simpler times. Oh how the years flew by, and we got to partake in all the experiences along the way. Mama's heart is full.

Put your marriage and family to the test; try that home project. Wear shorts and boots with confidence; you're rocking it! Learn to laugh, cuss, and farmer blow through the experience and move on. You can do this too; it makes the family stronger. It gets the creative juices flowing, and you may just get some new handy-dandy tools out of it. The experience adds great pride and appreciation to the whole adventure, and it brings back memories from years passed quickly. But most importantly, you create far more memories to share later.

We Are Under Construction

If you don't make the time to work
on creating the life you want,
you're eventually going to be forced
to spend a lot of time dealing
with a life you don't want.
—Kevin Ngo

We had entered a whole new phase of this wild adventure, and now decisions needed to be locked in. Put your seatbelts on because this is going to be a topsy-turvy ride for all involved. Overall, I knew the feel I wanted for The Zen Ranch. We were taking ideas from vacations where we had admired a certain style yet tweaking it a bit to what would accommodate the revolving door of our lively Timm boys and their posse. Trying to achieve this quest was quite the trip. Ryan did finally get those crisp white walls he had been requesting for years, and I complemented them with warm-gray trim to match the painted stone fireplace. Even the exterior sported his white, accented with extremely dark brown and metals (and now we see that everywhere). Rustic hickory lower kitchen cabinets were installed, topped with wood shelves on industrial hardware. A beachy sand, quartz shower, paired with matching vanity countertops were ordered with ease. Oh yes, that is corrugated metal on the bathroom walls. The industrial lighting fixtures were giddily brought home without a second thought. But dang, the entire house flooring and kitchen countertops were our drama queens. Our downtime was staring at samples, caressing samples, chauffeuring samples, rearranging samples, debating samples, and tripping over samples. It was a constant battle as all in the house had a say, well kind of, but I liked hearing their opinions anyway. The pressure was on—"Just pick out a damn sample, JennJenn!"

We had to take all the kids and fur babies coming and going into account when pondering these samples. What would be durable, what would hide the most, what would be super easy to clean, what would give off that away-on-vacation feel, and what would be freaking cool too? This process took time, as we needed to live with the sample—uh, samples. Multiple samples propped up in every corner of the house to view in all lighting morning, noon, and night, usually only to be returned a week later and a new batch selected to start the debate cycle all over again. Remember, there is a process to my madness! But it always works out beautifully in the end.

I have to admit, living in a house with all males does have its rewards, especially with my Timm men. I never do any heavy lifting and 99.5 percent of the time I tend to get catered to. I just bat my lashes or shed a tear and they jump, "JennJenn, we got you!" But when it came to needing help narrowing down a color, texture, sample, etc., *I so needed a female* in the house! This is a tiny example of what I had to work with:

> Evan: I don't care (strolls away).
> Ethan: I like that one! No, that one! Or, that one! Do you have more choices? (smart a$$)
> Ryan: (zeroing in) They all look the same. I have countertop fatigue.

Even if a non-Timm body slithered out of a room or up the stairs from their basement hideout, I grabbed them to add their opinion into the mix with their half-sleeping, squinting, blood-shot eyes and death stares as if saying, "JennJenn, just let me point, grunt, and go home please." I could always count on a few of them to give me full verbal opinions and legit interest, surprisingly mostly by Evan's squad. Darion, you were my design buddy on the detached garage. No maintenance, spot-on shade of cedar shake siding, perfecting the Cape Cod vibe. High five as we nailed that one in record timing—greatly appreciated! Now we can move on to the next thing on that list.

A remodel is really like a bunny hop. Projects may take days, weeks, full months, and sometimes—like in our case—a year or two, but slowly, progress is made. I would start each week with a goal to accomplish. No matter how big or small the task was, it was on my list, and my Ryan patiently waited for directions. Here's an ultimate example:

> ☐ Pick up a shower curtain rod and rings to hang new white waffle weave shower curtain in quartz

shower that isn't hooked up yet because the show-erhead I *want* doesn't seem to exist.

☐ I will repaint the window trim for the fourth time back to white because I have changed my mind on what is going on the adjacent walls—yes, again.

☐ I will get pine planks and leave them by Ryan's side of the bed until he decides to cut them and install them on the wall behind the toilet.

☐ Whitewash such installed planks.

☐ Well, this all can be accomplished after Ryan takes the drilled-in cement board down, behind the toilet, that is not needed since I have now decided I don't want tiled walls.

☐ Return such tile.

Make a freaking decision on
the entire house flooring!

He loves me, he loves me, he *must* because if I'm found dead, he's the *prime suspect,* and the whole town and all of social media knows it!

I'll use this opportunity to share something with you that normally I would not share. I know—me, right? But I figure, huh, this is my second book; we're invested in each other at this point, and honestly, many of you need to hear this, so here we go. We had a couple salesmen in the house pitching us on their must-have home products when one of the salesmen stopped and asked very curiously, "How long have you two been married?" We looked at each other and replied proudly in unison we were coming up on twenty-one years of marriage at that time. They were blown away, thinking we were newlyweds on a second marriage, still fresh in our single-digit years—completely shocked that we were doing a remodel while living in it, teenage boys coming and going, fur babies running about, while sitting there giggling and relaxed as can be with them. They were intrigued enough to ask what our secret to marriage was. We looked at each other silently rolling with laughter when Ryan gives me the adorable Timm wink. You know what, it wasn't always like this. There were some storms. There was one particular nasty storm that made us ready to throw in the towel many moons ago. When you're young, trying to get ahead, trying to build your career, trying to get the kiddos here, there, and everywhere, plus taking on way too much, you are drained to the core, which leads to stress, sharpness of the tongue, nasty eye beams toward each other, and extremely hurtful words do explode out. It happens to the best of us. A few times we were absolutely not on the same path. We did put ourselves in a timeout in different homes across town. You're thinking, *What? The Timms? No way!* Yes, *we Timms*! True story, bro. Girl, it happened! It was just a week, a very long week. Ethan was heartbroken his tribe was divided. I suspect he told every teacher, coach, and janitor within earshot. Evan didn't say a peep. We took the elders' advice and went to marriage counseling one time, and one time was all it took. What we learned in that single counseling trip was that particular counselor needed *us* for counseling. His marriage was more of a hot mess, train wreck, raving freakshow than we found ourselves in. Before the time was up, we were giggling, holding hands, and skipping our way out of the building. That session confirmed that we were just fine! We are going to be totally fine. All we needed was a pitstop to pull us back on track together. Maybe it was all an act by the counselor, but whatever, it worked. Give him a great review with five stars. We reminded ourselves to breathe, laugh, shake things off, and just move forward from there. Detour over. We were under construction a bit, we're cruising now—the worst is over!

Hey, you, fresh folks on this adventure, if you can just get through those grade school years, well the raving middle school years, oh, and those draining high school years with the kiddos and maybe, just maybe, get in some extra naps yourself, you are going to be just fine like my sackin' fish and I as we're in the honeymoon years of empty nesting as I write this book. Whew, we made it, super honored to still carry the title Mrs. Timm! Besides, he can't shake me off now. I'm his *forever*, as I need his medical insurance! Wink, wink.

Moving on the project list, and just like that, a whole entire freaking year flew by with projects being checked off our expanded taped-together to-do list, and we still had no floors throughout the majority of the house. But hey, we have upgraded the kitchen's splinter-giving plywood countertops to fabulous glossy-finish concrete. Check! The Zen Ranch custom grunge-stained subfloors with paint droppings and questionable character drawings by our eccentric Mr. Evan didn't seem to concern the Timm men much. Some families hung artwork on their refrigerators; we just aren't that kind of family! But new guests walking in raised an eyebrow while they gave a subtle glance around. I should have posted a disclaimer at the door: *"We are under construction. Ignore our dusty hot mess express. We have no idea what we are doing!"* I'll admit the management team had lost control and couldn't make a decision at that point. I guess we were following Evan's lead and just chillaxing. What's the urgency, right?

Sample after sample, the decisions, the possibilities—stop rushing me. What I want exists; I just know it, but where the heck is it? And then one glorious day, I get a call from a client to come to his body shop to discuss vinyl graphics, and our whole world was about to change by that request. Confidently walking into his shop—clipboard, camera, and tape measure in hand—I stopped abruptly, my heart skipped a beat, and my breath escaped me as his flooring called to me. It seduced me; the clouds opened, the sun shined down, and the angels sang—Houston, we had found the flooring of our dreams! The mismatched shades of grey, brown, and tan in a wood grain, porcelain tile, which was super easy to clean and disguised everything will be the perfect texture for my delicate feet. You are mine, all mine. I am so in love. I was patiently waiting for you. No, I did not get down on my knees and kiss it, nor did I roll around on it making snow angel motions. But now I'm wondering if I even met and accomplished the original request with the client because I had to rush to the store to lock in this flooring with a check ASAP!

I can't repeat this enough: find humor in your chaos. Be patient for what you want and dream about. Run ideas and plans by others. Brainstorming with the masses and cutting out the asses can lead you to a glorious and rewarding view. But first, do yourself a favor—take a nap and start fresh with a plan of action in a few hours. Your future self will thank you for it. Also, pat yourselves on the back if your marriage survived a remodel with more laughs, high fives, and hugs than cuss words, thrown hammers, and tears.

This Is Our Happy Place

If the simple things in life don't
put a smile on your face, then
you will never be truly happy.
—As seen on Pinterest

We are all in agreement that some of our most cherished years as a family were our camping days. A time for Dad to grill and our tribe to be outdoors from sunrise to sunset. We didn't need to go far to feel like we were away from it all and could sit back with our feet up in our hoodies, rubber boots, and elastic waist pants—matching attire was not required. Leaving makeup, work cell phones, and our laptops behind, eh, we didn't need a brush or really even a bra—let them breathe! It was Zen time—Jenn time with our camping gang. They all brought us year after year of wonderful memories. We lived outdoors those weekends, cooking and eating together on hard, uncomfortable picnic tables and loved every minute of it. All fur babies were welcome. Yes, even pampered Ryan, who hated bugs near him when eating,—we all were slowly breaking in this hotel city boy. We spent the days playing games together and the evenings around a firepit with many snort laughs. The fresh air was relaxing; welcomed and enjoyed. That was the life! We wanted to recreate that feeling once again at home, on The Zen Ranch.

It wasn't long after the purchase of The Zen Ranch when I left the office for a Zen time—Jenn time lunch at home. As I pulled onto the gravel driveway, I was greeted with quite the array of vehicles, from sports cars to dented trucks to supersized SUVs. It gave me a flashback to those overpriced and colorful bikes tossed in every direction not so long ago one summer afternoon in our previous house in town. My heart stopped a bit. Oh great, midday party at The Zen Ranch—awesome. I took that same deep sigh wondering what kind of lunch date this will bring, only to be oh-so-relieved to spot a good old-fashion game of whiffle ball in the oversized back lot with the end of the summer-hot sun beaming down on them. The large group of sweaty boys were laughing, slapping each other on the back, and putting others in a headlock. This continued to be the norm through the years at The Zen Ranch for boys of all ages. It felt so darn good, with a proud grin from ear to ear topped off with a glistening eye twinkle, that we gave them a safe and private space for boys to be boys, as loud as they wanted to be.

A whole school year later to start out the first official full summer on The Zen Ranch, our Mr. Evan had a bonfire for kids to toss in all their end-of-the-year schoolwork. The cars kept rolling in to drop off teenagers for the festivities. Ryan and I hung out in one of the garages to monitor who was coming and going. We were getting quite concerned on the growing number of bodies coming in on our dark road and the array of cars and trucks overtaking the lawn. Our anxiety reached another level when we learned they were posting out on social media for all to come join the shindig. We had Big-E and his "experienced" buddies do a few sweeps through when it got too dark for Ryan and I to spy. Well, now typing this a few years later, I feel this may have been a naïve mama move, but Ethan did incline to have the skill to tell us absolutely everything in full report-replay mode, and I'm surprised he didn't volunteer to take pictures to show us as well. (Oh, yes, honey, we have seen it *all* through the years.) We bet there were about fifty kids lounging around laughing, talking on the trampoline, playing with the dogs, snuggling up the kittens, and chilling to the music. High-five to those kiddos taking in the vibe of the property as we gave them a secure environment to be teenagers and to send their own smoke signals into town that, "School's out for summer!"

As soon as majority of the house to-do list was checked off and we were feeling we were in a good place, Ryan immediately focused in on what got him to move in the first place: the pool, the promised pool that he dreamt and envisioned back in our small corner lot in town. He found the perfect salesman who he could talk shop with, and in true Ryan fashion, go big or go home, he purchased the largest oval pool the dude had to offer. They agreed in unison that a partial inground pool is the way to go given our location, slope of the land, and placement to the house. Everyone was downright giddy with anticipation of the promised pool. It was game on with planning and watching the construction of this dream with a refreshment cooler stand purchased before swimming trunks and floaties even were a thought. Ryan got his pool that tipped this adventure into full-blown action. Work it pool boy. "Suns out guns out" quickly became his pool-cleaning time motto.

> *I'm going to admit it: I peed in the pool—more than once, shh... Come on, stop judging, I know many of you do this too. It's okay, I saw Ryan dumping plenty of chemicals in it to help. But curious, did anyone else wonder if a round colored ring would show up like they told us it would when we were younger in swimming lessons? I looked a few times. I don't think that is a real thing. Whew, feels good to be honest with you!*

Everyone wanted a piece of the Zen life at The Zen Ranch. We couldn't blame them. We created a pretty spectacular space. It was not unusual to pull onto the shaded driveway after work to be greeted with the lawn freshly mowed, trees trimmed, the scent of meat smoking, and one pretty darn relaxed, Timm dimple grin on a retired father-in-law floating in the now–super clean pool with music blaring, a cold one in his hand, and a few empties strategically lined the sides. Yes, I would say we could get use to this—a happy and free lawn boy, pool boy, master chef, and grocery delivery service for trade of pool time and the peaceful open scenery.

I'm naturally a planner. Strangely enough, many times I can be a wing-it girl, as everything always does work out in the end. So why on earth did I ever get my panties in a bunch? Breathe, JennJenn, breathe. As Ethan's senior year was approaching at top speed and we needed a game plan in place, I sent my Ryan out to that two-and-a-half car detached garage styling its new Cape Cod exterior. Ryan requested the wood barn entrance door to be painted a tropical turquoise. See how some color finally rubbed off on him? Only took twenty some years. Anyhoo, he was out there to get an idea if the space was doable for Big-E's graduation party. This building was used as a storage and grain shop for the previous owner's business for many years. I admit it needed a good cleaning and big imagination, but at this point, I needed level-headed Ryan to confirm it's a no-go before plan B was put in place. The day quickly passed and still no sightings of Ryan. It got me curious, so I ventured out to check on him. Jeez, now typing this years later, I realize that if there was an accident, it takes me most of the day to check if someone is okay in the family—oopsies, my bad! Well, something had happened that stopped me in my tracks. Umm, well, it turned out that a twelve-foot custom bar, three fifty-five-inch flat screen televisions, party lights, and oh wow, the previous owner already had a surround sound system hooked up was envisioned by this wonderful man of mine. So now we introduce *the Cave* to The Zen Ranch and became an additional living room space on the property with yet another fully stocked refrigerator. Apparently, we were a thirsty clan!

Now I personally thought the backyard paradise was the envy of the land, but when visitors stepped foot on the property, their stunned eyes and verbal awes proved that *the Cave* was the true gem—not just for what Ryan turned it in to, his own personal sports bar, but the structure itself. Apparently, they had wood envy, true wood envy. They would repeat, "You know this is true wood?" *The Cave* was constructed by actual wood from an original barn that was on the property at one time. Timber to barn build. Therefore, the walls and peak were built with overkill beams and support to stand to the ends of time. The constant wows confirmed to us that the interior wouldn't be closed in but shown off for all to see. The rustic majesty with patio heaters added to the rafters so the space could be utilized as much as we could year round, and boy, did they ever use it and abuse it!

And in my squirrel-like way on to another project, I just had to paint our propane tank. I mean it was dirty-white farm boring, so blah and depressing, glaring at me, taunting me, "JennJenn, I want a Zen Ranch makeover too!" Fair enough. So I gave all that were committed to the adventure narrowed down options: a chill pill, big watermelon, gigantic wiener, or big log. Those were the choices. All very fitting for what my life had become! Now the chill pill got many chuckles—because at this point of the adventure, I was thinking Prozac was needed for everyone around. Had I known about CBD oil at the time, that's what it would have been with no voting process. Gigantic wiener got many of the votes but would have been the hardest to tackle, and in reality, we would have quite the night crowd out from town to ride it. In all honesty, my sister just didn't need tempted when she visited as well. And big log because, well, I have boys, boys, and boys in the house, but was quickly crossed off the list due to the dark color on a propane tank may not be a wise choice. So my first watermelon of the season was masterly perfected and awesomely *ginormous*—the perfect, grand greeting to my garden.

Oh boy, did I have the green thumb! Thank you to the generous soil on the property, I proudly earned the name The Dirty Hoe. As soon as I pulled in the driveway from the workday, I tromped down to my garden in my heels, dress clothes, dangling earrings, and acrylic nails to play. As a few years passed, I found myself playing in the dirt in the morning before the beaming sun was high and my afternoons admiring my goods added to the Dirty Hoe produce stand out by the driveway for all to grab as they wish. Tips were appreciated—just shove those singles in! Oh, my melons were a glorious site and admired by all. Many would ask, "What's your secret, Dirty Hoe?"

"I just plant and walk away." Damn good soil on The Zen Ranch to grow big melons.

A demanding life continued outside The Zen Ranch property, but the minute we entered, it felt like we were far away from it all, living a fairy tale. Making our rounds to what all the property had to offer was a daily task. A soothing play in the dirt with my fur baby helpers before a refreshing strip and dip in the pool, letting the sun relax the day away. Lounging on the patio, feeling the soft evening breeze blowing away any worries, prior to walking the large lot, fur babies leading the march, to finding ourselves with our feet up on the firepit ledge, taking in the sky and the field view on the new upper deck. A perfect routine to settle in for the night. But as soon as the peaceful evening ended, we were right back to the grind among humans the next day. Ugh.

Here we are on our way out to work one fine summer, bird chirping morning only to be greeted with a sighting of handcuffs tossed by a pair of flipflops. Hmm, odd... Raising boys has resulted in some pretty bizarre finds—genitals drawn on dirty vehicle windows, clown wigs in back seats, extra clothing of all genders always in our laundry, but *this*, do I dare ask? Really, after a night of the Timm boys' midnight swimming with their posse, do we go back in to inquire to the slumbering boys or on to work we go? That is the question. Experienced boy mamas know just keep on walking; you don't want to know right now. Put a pin in that for later. And later in the day when it is brought up, both boys start beaming at each other and giggling, then the laughter tears appear with still no verbal explanations. You repeat, "I don't want to know. Just please, please, keep it to yourselves!" as I walk out the door to start my peaceful evening routine once again. Boys, you're in your twenties now, do I want to know yet? You both have careers that required background checks, so it must not have been too terribly concerning. We may just read about it in their own books someday!

Just like that, we were onto the years where our oldest, Big-E, left us to attend his first year away at college. We were thrilled about his plans and his own adventures, but I found the house was way too quiet. I was missing the rowdy crew hanging around, listening to their laughs, and the jabs and night-out stories. Suddenly, we had food in the house, no explosions in the microwave, no obnoxious parties in the pool until three o'clock in the morning, and no more mystery clothing in our laundry. Our land didn't look like a car lot, and our laundry had been reduced almost 70 percent. Boy did it suck! Although, we welcomed with wide arms the more frequent appearances from our Evan and his squad, which were sometimes larger in number but were chill and peaceful—well, at first!

Everyone needs their own time-out space to recharge to be able to tackle the humans in the world again. Create those spaces, create your playland, and create your ultimate paradise. Get down and dirty, strip and dip, let out your inner child, and be darn proud to show off your glorious big melons, dear!

This Is Our Happily Ever After, so We Thought

One day you'll wake up and there won't
be any more time to do the things
you've always wanted. Do it now.
—Paulo Coelho

Our fourth year on The Zen Ranch we had many break-ins around our community. Therefore, we decided to purchase a security camera with app to watch our property with alerts from anywhere and at any time. We could see when our Evan decided to leave for school and when he would roll in on the gravel during the evening hours after work. We could see when Ms. MirMar, our yellow lab, was roaming outside the fenced yard and when a delivery was made, plus where on earth they would leave the package this time. We even saw and enjoyed all the night critters that roamed near. We saw *everything*. It quickly became one of the greatest purchases we had made and gave us comfort and entertainment to watch every morning with our coffee as we caught the replay of the night show. And then Ethan found his way back home from college to heal from a second shoulder surgery. Initially, we felt pretty darn bummed for him to have had to leave his buddies and his baseball team to settle back home with his parents, but we quickly realized our 100 percent, all-in Ethan did receive a four-year college experience in nine months. He confirmed this his first month away from home when Ryan and I felt the urge to drive up to check-in on him and ask how he was doing, only to be greeted with a dramatic swing-his-head-back deep chuckle and in full E enthusiasm, "You thought I peaked in high school, I'm killing it here!" Oh, sweet baby Jesus, why did we ever worry about this one? Anyhoo, he was back home with us now. He quickly moved his brother upstairs again and turned our basement into his own walk-out apartment complete with a living room, bedroom, bathroom, and his own kitchen. We only had to share a laundry room and storage room with him. He had quite the adult setup, and we were pretty darn happy to have him home again and to give him his own space. A separate space away from us. But umm, guys, his never-ending entourage, as you all were coming and going from his own entrance, we could see you peeing on our fence outside our home. There was a camera *right there*! We did accommodate him with his own cool, cabin-industrial bathroom with a sink to wash your tally-whacker-touched hands! Morning coffee giggles on The Zen Ranch were always topped off with a, "What the hell is wrong with them?" shake of the head.

The summer Ethan moved back home was Evan's start to his senior year, which by then, he decided to fast track through school and graduate early, thank God! I was transitioning from a full-time career to part-time and enjoying some peaceful, stress-free afternoons at home when Ethan and his adorable college girlfriend decided they just couldn't stand the miles apart, and she would be joining us on The Zen Ranch in his basement apartment together. She fit into our tribe like a glove. She was sweet and sassy, just the way we needed her to be to settle in with us. It was wonderful having another female in the house and one that matched up perfectly to tame our Ethan, include our Evan on lunch dates, love on our fur babies, and talk sports with Ryan. Even though she showed up in his *Cave* with a Packers jersey and sparkling smile proudly on one awkward Viking game day family gathering. Yes, bold and sassy is our Jana; Ethan did good! She sealed the deal for me when she left on the kitchen counter a smashed vape apprentice, a hammer, and a note, "This is *not* a house that *juuls*!" I had no idea what a *juul* was, but if she says so, then we certainly were not such a house! I freaking love her! Therefore, more plans were set in motion to accommodate all of us living together in harmony, including their newly adopted coonhound mix puppy, Ozo—*surprise*! Yes, if you are counting from my previous book, that is now *five* fur babies under one roof! Poop patrol was a grand daily chore and thank goodness for tiled flooring. The fabulous tiled flooring I waited so long for.

Before we knew it, a whole year flew on by with this new arrangement, and I officially had left the workforce to welcome Zen time—Jenn time at home every day, all day. (Hold tight, you will learn soon enough why.) Evan had finally marked off his school career. We triple-checked to be sure. The longest pre-K through 12 ever! *Whew,* we made it! And he quickly secured himself full-time employment. Ryan was working from home more and more. Ethan and Jana found themselves full-time positions locally, and *no one* seemed to have any plans to leave our family paradise. Therefore, a separate structure was brainstormed, drawn up, priced out, and jumped through hoops to get this city or that city approval back and forth, back and forth. Come on, just accommodate our desire to have our own space and get some solid sleep at night, for Ryan and I, please, I beg you! I mean really, the boys entourage and squad are night owls, baking pizzas in our oven at 3:00 a.m. with an ungodly amount of extra bodies in and out of the pool, the surrounding basketball court–patio and *the Cave,* "Oh my gosh, who is screaming?" while we are trying to get our beauty sleep with five fur babies in the house barking in full disapproval that they, too, have had it with this, "We are set in a vacation-time lifestyle. Seriously, is that the smoke alarm again, and how the hell does tomato sauce get on the ceiling?" One Mississippi, two Mississippi…sigh.

I remember one time, my mother said, "She was done parenting. She was just over it." With all stunned, weird feelings, I thought, *What the hell, mother! How could you say that—you're my mom!* And then here we are, many years later, we're in the same boat with the exact same feelings. I totally get it completely. High five, pat yourself on the back. How the steaming hell did you do it with three wild Collins kids whom two were girls, fourteen months apart— enlarged, shocked, stunned eye stare—when Dad was over it years before you? Give yourself a Colorado brownie and put a crown on because you're a freaking queen. No more snowflake offense here; *I get it now*!

The Zen Ranch served its purpose for the Timm boys' teen years. Many fond memories and what-the-hell moments were made. We provided a safe environment for the boys' friends to be typical teenagers in peace. Well, we certainly tried at least. There were a few fireworks shot at kids floating in the pool who were actually encouraging it, while Ryan and I were furiously screaming, "Are you an idiot?" along with a few trees backed into by fancy little sports cars. A kid camped out on the roof then in a tree in the middle of the darn night seemed a bit like an R-rated movie we watched. Anyhoo, deep breath. We once thought The Zen Ranch was going to be our forever home, our happily ever after, a property past down to our boys someday. But they just wouldn't move out, and the stove needed a deep clean from all those late-night, umm, early morning munchies. The new stainless-steel refrigerator was dented and scratched up, so let's make it simple for you: your father and I decided to sell it all and move out of town to our own fresh, new, quiet townhome instead. *Boom!*

Life changes; it changes suddenly and a bit abruptly, which gets you thinking and reviewing. Speed bumps were sprung on us, and detours appeared. What once was my outdoor paradise living room and my utter joy to be The Dirty Hoe of The Zen Ranch has now become an emotional burden, not at all Zen time–Jenn time anymore. New neighborhood developments were moving in on our once-open field views. Plus, we all were in agreement we were getting on one another's nerves a tad. It was time.

Time for some major changes, a bit more distance apart. It may have been escalated when I walked out of my own bedroom one morning without pants and was greeted with "Ew, put some pants on!" which was equally matched with an "Ew, move out, get your own place!" as I smirked and strolled on down the hallway into the kitchen to my morning bliss of coffee to save my day with the tune of our wedding exit song playing in the background of my head,

> Zip-a-dee-doo-dah, zip-a-dee-ay
> My, oh, my, what a wonderful day
> Plenty of sunshine headin' my way
> Zip-a-dee-doo-dah, zip-a-dee-ay!

> (Fun fact and to cover my butt, per Google, song was composed by Allie Wrubel with lyrics by Ray Gilbert for the Disney 1946 live action and animated movie *Song of the South*, sung by James Baskett.)

Jeez, relax, everyone. Everything was covered. By the way, pants are and have always been overrated—let 'em breathe, let it all breathe!

> *Fly, my Timm boys, be that peacock! You have made us super proud, and you are ready. It's time for JennJenn to just be a stay-at-home dog mom now. But remember, always make good choices!*

Now I know many of you parents are reading this going "Yes! Yes! Yes! I know the feeling!" while others who are still fresh in the honeymoon stage of parenting are thinking, as I once was, *What the hell, what kind of mother thinks that?* Oh, honey, you're so adorable. You will get there. Come vent to me when it hits you. Here's my experienced mama hint: it will hit! But in the meantime, breathe through it; you will get through it. Just walk around your house without pants on and maybe even put a *For Sale* sign front and center in your lawn as it will help speed the whole process up. You're so welcome for the advice. Now make those plans on what is to come when you have your partner all to yourself again. Oh, the possibilities! You're feeling all warm and fuzzy now, huh? *What an amazing adventure it has all been*, you will think calmly and proudly to yourself.

Day of Purchase.

Tada!

Before the tear out of closet begun.

Tada!

Day of purchase.

Tada!

Day of purchase.

Tada!

Back porch before and after.

It's All Fun and Games Until Someone Gets Sick

Finding the Humor, Blessings, and Lessons in Our Journey

Adventure 2.5

Adventure 2.5

To our Ethan, we are in awe of you—how you tackle life with your ginormous grin and showing those dimples through your years, how you have educated your peers of what gluten is and what it does to your body, how you soared through your adolescence with grace when in pain and developed strong coping skills while dealing with a nasty disease. We love you to pieces for giving us the strength to buck up on this journey because, well, we Timms have plans for ourselves and can't let anything hold us back too long. You, my boy, inspire me to keep trucking forward. Let's keep this rolling!

Mom asked me once, "What do you say when people ask about your dad?" It was a serious yet blank question. I mean, what are we to say—"He's doing great!" which he is, but in actuality, the guy has battled five different cancers for over twenty years, yet he hardly missed a day of work. Chemo, radiation, toxic pills, surgery, immunotherapy shots and IVs—shots that could kill a horse, yet the guy put on a smile and was trucking through because he has responsibilities and people relying on him. The doctors said, "He is the unluckiest and luckiest man alive. Not sure how he's alive, but alive..." But what do we say? One good friend puts it best, simply stating, "He's Dennis Collins—he's a badass!"

To my *badass* dad, you have worked hard for us all and played hard with us all. It's time to relax, put your feet up, and enjoy it all! This book is for you, as you have given me so much strength and guidance to keep going—work hard, battle hard; it can always be worse.

Two Foreign Words

Ethan, Ethan, Ethan, you
poor, sick bastard…
—Ryan Timm, Dad

I'm going to start in a bit harsh. I'm just going to say it and get it over with like ripping off a Band-Aid quickly; do not drop your jaw and judge quite yet. Please give me time to explain. Here we go: it has not been easy living with our Ethan, period. Not at all. It just hasn't. It's been exhausting, frustrating, expensive, emotional, at times embarrassing, and oh so demanding. When he was a baby, we would take him to the doctor (often) to be told he's just fussy, colicky, or has gas—"Here, give him these drops to help his tummy." Then we would run him back again to the doctor to be told he's lactose intolerant. They would suggest a change to a make-us-barf-from-the-smell-of-it specialty formula, a formula that would be thrown up most of the time. When he was a toddler, we would take him in to be seen because his stomach was hard and protruding balanced on little chicken legs, only to be told he's gassy or on many, many occasions, "We don't need to swab him. We can tell by looking down his throat, he has strep." I would run him constantly to the doctor's office because of the extreme gas pains causing him to be, on all fours, rocking back and forth holding his stomach. Irritable bowel syndrome was mentioned a few times. They poked him and had us running all over, doing tests with vague answers. The day I was told by our annoyed family doctor, "Mrs. Timm, sometimes, children just have upset stomachs," because once again, this naïve young mother was back in his office with her son. Oh, buddy, did you just poke the wrong mama, who has quite the determination in her to get answers and well, he just stirred the damn dragon!

This was during a time I was starting to get involved with a small church when I found myself venting at a Bible study out of pure exhausted frustration from a day of testing with the poor boy, knowing the next morning they were going to continue with tests when a kind lady grabbed my arm and instructed me exactly, word for word, what blood work needed to be requested or demanded to be done and where to send it. Here we go again. That annoyed family doctor started the day glaring at me as I was telling him how to do his job and what tests needed to be performed, "Dude, humor me and just run the darn test that I am paying for!" The lab came back with a diagnosis, two foreign words were written down, and just like that, we were finally sent on our way to a specialist, where a scope was performed to reveal such damage that our poor Ethan had lesions coming up his throat. Umm, not *strep*—lesions, sores from the years of damage in his stomach because even the annoyed doctor had no idea what this disease entailed way back then. Whew, finally some answers, and we can cross that family doctor off our list for good and move on to a more informed, understanding specialist. My coworker at the time disgustingly announced, "They are just practicing medicine," which I totally understood after seven whole years of this "practicing" at the expense of our pocketbook and used up personal time off, thank you very much. I would like all our copays back now sir!

The two foreign words, *Celiac Sprue*, will forever change our lives. If you Google "Celiac Sprue Disease," this is what you will find as the description: *Celiac disease, sometimes called celiac sprue or gluten-sensitive enteropathy, is an immune reaction to eating gluten, a protein found in wheat, barley and rye. If you have celiac disease, eating gluten triggers an immune response in your small intestine. Over time, this reaction damages your small intestine's lining and prevents it from absorbing some nutrients (malabsorption). The intestinal damage often causes diarrhea, fatigue, weight loss, bloating and anemia, and can lead to serious complications. In children, malabsorption can affect growth and development, besides causing the symptoms seen in adults. There's no cure for celiac disease—but for most people, following a strict gluten-free diet can help manage symptoms and promote intestinal healing.*

If you ask Ryan and I, we will explain, *gluten is the devil that causes havoc in a celiac body. It's like a poisonous monster fighting to get out; however, it possibly can and sets a fire on anything in its way. It reacts differently within every* celiac; therefore, it is hard to diagnose unless a scope is performed. Blood work doesn't always confirm it. It's an expensive and frustrating life-altering diagnosis.

In Ethan's words, *"Growing up with celiac disease was hard at first. Having stomach pains every second of the day at such a young age and not knowing why or how it is happening really threw my life off. Vomiting and always visiting the bathroom of any home, school, or business, I was getting to the point of not knowing how to live a healthy life. I had years of pain that affected my stomach and felt bloated all day. I had chest pains that would make me fall completely to the ground, like a ten-pound weight had fallen on me, begging for it to go away. I had nonstop shaking through my whole body that I had no control over. Also, headaches that would sometimes drag me to my bed for hours, leaving me to lie there in complete darkness and sometimes passing out. Many effects from celiac disease took place in my early years of life. Most were so painful that I would never wish them on my worst enemies. Celiac disease is a scary disease to have especially when you don't know what is wrong with you. So when people ask me what is your opinion on celiac disease, I tell them, 'You may feel you are living a life lesson of pain and suffering, but through all of it, learn to not take life for granted but to be thankful for what you have and keep fighting the long, hard, and tiring battles.' Because someday, you will look back at what makes you who you are, and you will be thankful for all the blessings in your life."*

Gosh, we adore him!

With this new confirmed diagnosis, we were pointed in the right direction with some real answers to get our boy feeling better. Our mission was to get his stomach down, to get him gaining some weight to match up to his peers, and to get his bowels under control. We must get this poor child feeling his best and out of pain. The specialist's nurse printed off on a low-toner printer the appropriate food lists, the description of this foreign disease, and off to home we went. We quickly realized *everything* in the freaking home and the activities we attended and at his elementary school were making him sick! *We were making him sick*—for seven whole years! My heart broke. Ryan and I held each other teary-eyed, exhausted, shattered, and lost. *What do we do?* No one seems to know what this is or what gluten is. How do we fix this? How do we explain this? How do we keep him safe? Thankfully, our new church friend dropped everything to come to our rescue with years of experience with this disease. She took us to the grocery store to show us labels and what we needed to search for. Back then in 2005, it wasn't the law to have allergen ingredients separated out and in bold like we are blessed to have nowadays on our food packages. How very "lovely" for the newbies who didn't have an experienced friend to guide them through this hiccup. (That was sarcasm if you didn't pick that up.) We had to dissect every label every single time because, depending on where and when the food was processed, the contamination and ingredients varied—how freaking awesome was that! (Again, sarcasm here, folks!) This was all before we just decided a plain and simple farmer's diet of unseasoned meat and vegetables would become our signature diet. We heard, "Is a potato gluten?" more times than we can count. No one knew this strange word! (I'll save you time looking it up; a potato is not gluten. It is a safe vegetable.)

> *I'll admit, in the beginning, before I fully committed to the gluten-free lifestyle, I would grab our non-celiac Evan to do "errands" so we could devour a gluten foot-long at the local sub shop because I'm that type of mom. I would never do now because I, too, realize and feel the effects. Gluten is the devil, but at the time, it was quite the struggle to break off the nasty relationship.*

We did get steered toward a support group those first few months where everyone around us had a completely different journey to their celiac diagnosis—from bloated purging to rail thin, sick bodies to cancer diagnosis from years of damage to a young dark-haired boy going bald, as his only symptom due to the malnourishment caused by the disease. How scary that had to be for those parents and that young child!

The lesson learned is, listen to your body. When a four-year-old asks for a salad, like our Ethan always did, then that's what you give—hold the croutons. When your body wants a burger with no bun, then don't fight it. When you receive a diagnosis that doesn't feel right, you keep pushing for more answers, stand your ground! Tom Petty's soul speaks to me in his song "I Won't Back Down" with his lyrics,

No, I'll stand my ground
Won't be turned around
And I'll keep this world from draggin' me down
Gonna stand my ground
And I won't back down
Hey, baby there ain't no easy way out
Hey, I will stand my ground
And I won't back down
Well, I know what's right
I got just one life
In a world that keeps on pushin' me around
But I'll stand my ground
And I won't back down

The Purge

It's coming out one way or the other...
—Ethan's Daily Life

The supersized story-and-a-half house and Ethan's diet were stripped of gluten, but as we were stumbling through how to handle contamination to gluten from surfaces or outside the home, we found putting this seven-year-old boy in a bathtub would settle his tummy and body aches a tad. Going to the floor on all fours rocking back and forth with Lamaze breathing and strange grunts seemed to help. Having him lean back on us so we could rub his swollen belly in a circular motion would ease the pain a bit. These practices would usually calm the battle within him until he could sleep it off or just let time run its course for the gluten to exit his body. Although there was one particular time we tried everything to help soothe him with no luck; he was in excruciating pain, so we rushed him to the ER. As the physician on duty was poking away at his protruding, hard, swollen belly, Ethan was grunting in horrible pain when the physician looked at us and pronounced, "He is entirely backed up," which stunned us because the boy was purging numerous times a day all week long. They insisted he needed an enema to clean him out and give him some relief right now. An enema? What the heck? Well, I guess, if you say so, sign him up. Let's do this enema thing. We're game to help the poor boy however we can!

We stood in the cramped room to watch this in action step by step. We tried our best to console the hurting, now panicking, child as we assisted in rolling him over and rubbed his back to relax. Relax? Um, something was going up an area where nothing should be going up ever! But we reassured the best we could, having no experience ourselves with such matters.

"Ethan, you need to relax. Let them do what they need to do," I pleaded, as I held his little hands. He was arching and frantically screeching, "What are they doing back there? What are they doing?" and again, Ryan and I repeated trying not to laugh, cry, or run from the scene, "Honey, relax, they need to do this." Louder and louder, screaming echoed through the room and down the hall, "But what are they doing, what is that? *Stop!*" as he was reaching back trying to stop them before Ryan had to hold him down with full force as they inserted the tube.

Talk about a horribly awkward, uncomfortable feeling to do to your child who was already in pain. I just wanted to grab my boy and run far away with him. Ryan and I had never had an enema in our life, so we had no idea what the feeling was. Then they told him he had to lay there on the table with this liquid squirted up his plugged bottom and wait five minutes. Five minutes! Ethan jumped off that table the second Ryan released his hold on him. He started screaming even louder and crazier, holding his bottom, "I got to go! I got to go!" And the nurse calmly said, "You have to wait. You have to wait the entire five minutes." Ryan and I were trying our best not to lose our shit watching this all go down—this circus, this train wreck—as the nurses backed out of the room. I'm sure they were trying to contain their own laughter or annoyance as they now had to go assure the neighboring rooms that they were not torturing a child.

Ethan proceeded to pace back and forth begging and pleading, "I got to go, I got to go," still holding his bottom side with his gown fully open. We're sounding like a broken record now—"Buddy, you have to wait. You have to wait the full five minutes like they said." Ryan and I impatiently looked all around, up the hallway, down the hallway. What in tarnation do we do? Try not to laugh, try to take a deep breath, and try not to cry in frustration for him. This poor boy was in pain with a swollen belly, now feeling like he has lost complete trust in us as the wise parents, as he was screaming and climbing the walls and holding his bottom side. By now, the nurses were huddled together giggling in the hallway as this screaming child was frantically and wildly running around the room in desperation, "It's coming, it's coming! I can't hold it any longer!"

They finally appeared with their stopwatch and said, "Okay, you can now go." Ethan hollers at them wide eyed and frantic, "Go? Where can I go, where do I go?" The nurse just calmly points down the hallway. Oh, for shit's sakes, he now has to run down the hallway? Gown open to the world, his hands on his bare bottom, Ethan took off in a full-on sprint, hurdling everything in his sight, as if he's a determined linebacker on a football field, still screeching for the whole hospital and half of Iowa to hear, "It's coming! It's coming!" With an assortment of low, shuddered concerned breaths and pushing his way through the door of the restroom, he finally could explode in relief. I don't think that poor child even gave a rat's ass if the door made it shut, while we all stood in the hallway making relieved and awkward shy glances all around to the other patients and visitors now peeking from their own emergency rooms out of concern. Someone missed an award-winning comical video here! Whew, we made it through that one—barely.

Now traveling with Ethan wasn't the easiest either. Those darn food labels still didn't have the allergy listing clearly posted in bold text like we are blessed with these days. We had to study labels and look for words we recognized on these foreign ingredients. We got pretty darn good at it and mainly kept to a handful of brands that we knew were safe. Away on an Ozark vacay with a family who we had grown close to through the years in the neighborhood gang days, our then–grade schooler Ethan was all about a grilled hotdog, and we felt confident it was pretty safe to let him devour after looking over the package thoroughly, watching closely the grill master's tongs at work and that the grilled wieners were far away from the gluten buns for the rest of the party. But boy, oh boy, were we severely wrong! Within twenty minutes, Ethan jumped to his feet screaming and running frantically with all kinds of grunts and heavy breathing to slam the bathroom door in the condo, releasing an explosion of bathroom scary sounds. To give you a more accurate image, have you seen the bathroom scene in *Dumb and Dumber*? Yeah, you get it a bit now. Okay, but add a bit more Ethan-dramatics. As the concerned mama, I was standing outside the door asking if he needed help ("Please say no, please say no," repeated in my head) when he awkwardly said, "Uh, I need you." Whew, wee, it was a horror show of poo-blast everywhere the eye could see! Pink rug on the floor to the side, dusty mauve shower curtain, to the wall behind him and up his back was all the evidence that the gluten contaminated food didn't agree with his stubborn body. Oh, sweet Lord, the spicy wiener smell was horrendous, and nothing in view could be used to pinch my nose tightly closed. Poor E, he looked so terribly exhausted and obviously thoroughly drained on the destroyed stool. All while the neighboring, concerned mama was standing in the hallway asking through the door what she could do to help. Bleach, plastic bags, gloves, and any other murder scene cover-up supplies you can find is what is needed and needed fast—oh, and fresh clothing! Should we just gut the room and let your contractor husband rebuild it on his vacation?

As the mamas were on the cleanup, scrub-down crew, my-go-with-the-flow and accommodating Evan sat happy as a clam eating his grilled spicy hotdog in a gluten bun out on the patio with the two dads sucking down their brews oblivious to the bathroom fiasco. Well, on the plus side, at least the condo owners' sixties bathroom decor got updated to 2010 when we checked out. This gal got to do some updating—I like leaving my touch everywhere I go!

The holidays—oh, the fabulous holidays seemed to bring on a new form of stress during our everyday lives. For many, it meant exciting travel plans and glorious menu ideas. For a celiac family, it meant alternative meal prep and packing emergency spare bottoms. It also meant for us, the Timms, a two-and-half-hour trip to Papa's Farm turned into a five-hour trip with a middle schooler hanging his bare buns out of our truck door in the middle of the freezing winter on the side of the road because we were already ten miles away from the last restroom stop that he demolished a toilet in. All while the super annoyed non-celiac younger brother was snuggled in with blankets and his video game, just wanting to get to Grandma's house to see what was waiting for him under the tree. With all our napkins from the glove box quickly used up, Ryan and I exhaustedly debated, do we just turn around and head home? But we're already too invested in the trip. The bone-tired, past-embarrassed middle schooler announced, "This family Christmas better be worth it," as we call ahead to say our arrival is delayed again. Entertaining the extended family was what we did in those days. We all still giggle about it, and now shall you. Well, did you get the picture why our Big-E was so little? He purged about anything that got in him with his temperamental body.

Soon we were parents of teenagers. Ryan and I found ourselves having alone time more and more on The Zen Ranch, which was wonderful and welcomed. It gave us time to catch up, but it always steered back to our main life topic. Sitting around our living room laughing about how we would have been a hit reality show, reminiscing about all the Timm bros situations through the years that we just couldn't make up. "No one would actually believe this went down" seemed to be the Timm motto. This just couldn't be normal family daily events when we were startled by the back door flying open abruptly, and there's Ethan bursting through the door screeching in a high pitch, "I need to take a dump! I need to take a dump now! Oh, it's coming! It's coming now! I can feel it!" as his loud commentary was diminishing as he went down the hallway.

I'm matching his screaming and wailing my arms around demanding, "Not our bathroom! Not our bathroom! Go downstairs to yours!" All while Ryan sat stunned, annoyingly staring at me and wide eyed. Then slowly, he raised his stiff arm up, giving direction to our Ethan, with no verbal words to say as we both know. Here is another perfect example of Timm life, or I'm ever so hoping life with boys in every family. Please, boy mamas, please tell me this is normal: do they all really need to go this much and feel the need to announce it out loud every single time?

I'll leave you with a repeat of our Ethan's words: "*You may feel you are living a life lesson of pain and suffering, but through all of it, learn to not take life for granted but to be thankful for what you have and keep fighting the long, hard, and tiring battles. Because someday, you will look back at what makes you who you are and you will be thankful for all the blessings in your life.*"

Living with a Celiac

Not all storms come to disrupt your
life, some come to clear your path.
—Unknown

As many young mamas got to enjoy trips to Jamboree groups or fast-food playlands with their tribe, I got to be glamorously treated to visits to the GI office and shut in the room with all my Timm men to stare at a rather supersized poop chart. Our daily life consisted of poop discussions according to this disgusting but this-is-our-reality-to-compare-to chart. How lucky for me! I don't remember any discussions in school, my own parents' home, or from friends to prepare me that part of a marriage or raising a family was knowing in detail, and I mean in absolute detail—what the timing, amount, color, texture, shape, and frequency of your bowel movements should be. And no, boys, I do not need a picture of your purge. Just give me a thumbs up all is good according to the doc and go about your activities, please and thank you. Really, Ryan, I don't remember the doctor requesting you to report either. Be jealous, ladies, of my classy life!

As normal siblings do, one will always pick a fight with their sibling when there is too much down time. But with boys, it seems it turns into a full-blown wrestling match, no matter where or when. Of course, for us, the older one, the stronger one at the time, seemed to always take it way too far, which would leave the younger, smaller one in tears. Our non-celiac Evan, who seriously ponders things through entirely and takes in every situation in silence to make his next move, got the final last laugh one particular time when we had gluten in the house for a special occasion for our guest. His ninja movements went into action as he grabbed up a gluten oyster cracker sack ("Ha, ha," she said, "sack!" Sorry, been around boys too much) and pounced upstairs to their bedroom level. He proceeded to strategically place the gluten in between Ethan's bedsheets. So when Big-E was greeted at bedtime, there was gluten contamination everywhere, and we heard Evan trying to contain his giggling from the next room. That boy learned to quietly conquer leaving a permanent mark to remember through the years so Ethan would leave him the hell alone out of fear of what that spider ninja would do next. This one left Ryan and I struggling whether we should scold, punish, turn our backs and laugh, high-five in epic payback, or lock our own bedroom doors at night.

In the earlier celiac years of adapting to the gluten-free lifestyle, there were times Ethan would get into some cross contamination. Whether it was just a little bit or a lot, his reactions seemed to go in cycles of purging, upset stomach, flu-like feelings, or complete emotional, blow out–freak outs. It varied and there was no warning. Let's just say we didn't have to pay for much entertainment in those years because we could count on Ethan to give us a grand show.

The most memorable Oscar-worthy performance of them all, leaving Evan with laughter tears streaming down his face every single time he replays the scene, even to this day as a twenty-year-old. Evan replays the incident:

> Out of nowhere, Ethan just started crying and accusing us of different things (head tilted back, body shake laughter).

> He kept yelling at us and wasn't making sense (hands to his face wiping away laughter tears).

> He got so mad and twitching he didn't know what to do with himself, so he grabbed the closest thing, a bar stool, and raised it over his head, like the Incredible Hulk, with a vein bulging in his neck (full on-air laughing, eyes closed with tears rolling out).

> Mom and I just looked at each other like, what the hell? Half hour later, after getting him safely in his room to calm down and lie down, Ethan appeared again in the kitchen and announced, "Well, that was embarrassing!" (outright laughter)

> And to this day, we still don't know what got him so worked up (wiping face with more deep laughter)!

This may be the only thing Evan has ever shown complete *Ethan enthusiasm* in retelling a story. Poor Ethan, you really had no control over that darn body!

Not only did Big-E have to deal with stomach and bowel issues but he regularly was dealing with bladder, breathing, and polyp issues throughout his teen years. The joys of this disease caused many oddities in his body due to the years of damage and malnutrition. We reminded him regularly and quite harshly, "We aren't treating you special because of this. This is your life, and we can't let it affect school, activities, and your plans for yourself." We dealt with it as it came and moved on. We reminded him this is doable and can always be worse, so do what the doctors say and get on with your business. We had to, as we hoped it would make him stronger and not cater, or baby, this life hiccup. No victims here. But I must admit, looking back, it was hard putting up that front when I just wanted to grab him, coddle him, protect him, and run away with him. Also admittedly, at times, we wanted to grab him, shake him, beat him, and send him away. It was a constant struggle.

You see, when you mix a hormonal, lack-of-sleep teenager with a handful of new toxic prescriptions, including an anxious, powerful side-effect steroid combined with a hyper, stressed-to-the-max-from-work, insomniac mother after a pot of steaming, strong black coffee, with no food in her tummy and a father who stayed up late for the teenager to return home from his friends equals an awesome party in the Timm home! After week one of the toxic prescriptions, we were all still standing; "We can do this" was repeated often. Damn, why couldn't CBD oil have been available to us during these years; our life would have been so much more balanced, chill, and handled smoothly. Well, this book was produced many years later, so obviously, all survived; we can conquer all together—*booyah*!

Word traveled fast in our small community (got to love a small community). The school district promptly put in place a gluten-free food program and assigned an area of the kitchen just for him, his own assigned food tray and his own on-top-of-it-all cook. Families started educating themselves, and warnings were finally starting to be put on food labels for allergies across the country. Restaurants were recognizing they needed to offer alternative menus, and education on the topic of gluten was becoming mainstream, which led us to be contacted by the local community magazine to do an article on *"A New Way of Eating."* I spent an hour and a half on the phone with the local journalist covering all her questions. I added my insight on issues she never even thought of with celiac disease, gluten, what it does to the body, and any concerns we had as parents at the time with our high schooler. As one of the first recognized celiac in our family doctor's office and one of a few in our school district, we were full of knowledge from our research and experiences along the journey. We were honored that we were the family who was picked for the cover and interviewed for the article. After all we had been through, it was nice to have a little rewarded spotlight. So when I actually go to read the printed article, it was pretty darn good as it picked up on some fine highlights, but I chuckled hard when it was brought up,

As Ethan has gotten older, his parents have discussed the risks of drinking and the repercussions of having a beer with gluten in it. His health depends on him remaining vigilant with his diet, as he has had ongoing health issues tied to his exposure to gluten from infancy.

That was my addition to the article as a mother of sixteen- and fourteen-year-old sons at the time. Out of everything we discussed as a concern—eating out in restaurants, what to look for on menus, to speak to a manager or cook on duty, having a safe alternative snack handy for him with classroom parties, having a strong rapport with school nurses, janitors, and cooks on safe foods and surface prep for cross contaminations—but no, the ending quote showed our main concern: whether our boy could have a beer with his buddies! Parenting at its best, "Oh those Timms, just concerned about their liquid diet!" Hand to the face, shaking my head, roll of the eyes. Ethan, how are things going now as you made it through those later high school and college years with a few of those "peer-pressured" beers? Whew, we're all learning from setbacks, paying attention, and unfortunate reminders why we just can't have gluten in our bodies at all, no matter what others are doing. Priorities are by unfortunate lessons learned behind closed doors. Thank goodness you have a determined girl on your arms to firmly remind you now that Mama isn't in your space.

I read once when a family member is chronically ill, the whole family is sick. Oh boy, that is so true. Everyone is sick and tired with worry—sick and tired of the constant testing and the waiting game, sick and tired of all the changes in the home, sick and tired that this is our life now, sick and tired this is even happening to them, sick and tired of the financial burden, and what was once a smooth-traveled road has become extremely bumpy and a bit disturbing. Although, what I have learned—and I'm sure you are even noticing in your own family hiccups—you become a stronger, tighter family unit with coping skills that will serve you well in life and that these little speed bumps in the journey open your view to become much more appreciative to the good in your life. Wouldn't you agree, with a little bit of an eye roll, smirk of the mouth, and shrug of a shoulder, that you are a stronger animal because of what you have gone through and that you can handle anything tossed at you on this journey?

Yes, calm down, I received permission to use this photo.

Oh for Shit's Sakes

I truly believe that every single person
has to go through something that
absolutely destroys them so they can
figure out who they really are.
                                    —Unknown

Disclaimer: There are a lot of cuss words in this chapter. The emotions were high at the time, so if you have virgin ears, simply skip over it. But in some situations, there are no other words that are fitting, and cuss words are extremely called for. By the way, there are many articles, statics, and studies proving people that curse a lot have higher intelligence, have better vocabularies, make better friends, and are simply happier human beings. It's true. Google it. Boy, oh boy, are some of you freaking laid back, friendly "geniuses"! So we're just going to let it rip in this chapter, okay? Here we go.

My curious, always-getting-us-pondering, educated, prudent, retired-schoolteacher mother once asked each of us three adult kids, "What is your what-the-fuck moment?" Oh, dear Lord, where would I even begin, as I take a deep breath with about a thousand life moments flashing in front of my eyes. I tear up, chuckle, and must tame the dragon with emotional moments that came to me strongly with this question. I mean, Ethan's celiac came to mind, but really, that was just a shitty time.

One ridiculous WTF example that stands out front and center was, for years, we had been wanting to get away for a nice, all-inclusive tropical vacation. Everyone else was doing it. We heard their stories; we saw their pictures, and we constantly said we shall do this too. But there were always distractions and schedule conflicts or reasons why we didn't book the trip. With our *big* year upon us of— yeah, we made it to—Ethan's senior year of high school, continuing the celebration of my fortieth birthday, and our upcoming twentieth wedding anniversary, we were excited that we were going to spend spring break in Riviera Maya, Mexico, at an all-inclusive, dreamy tropical resort. The week prior, multiple vials of blood work came back with red flags across the board, and I was diagnosed with this nasty, hideous word *lupus*. Stop the freaking truck, say what? Now? WTF! I was given the greenlight to continue with our vacation plans but firmly instructed to stay out of the sun, get plenty of rest, take the handfuls of colorful toxic prescriptions daily, and told to report back for more rounds of testing and biopsies promptly when we return to the states. *Yep*, we have to shake our heads, ugly cry, and hysterical laugh all at once. So while Ryan was drinking it up and frying in the sun, I had customized my plans to chill in a hammock under a tree or in a cabana, fully covered, with my brimmed hat, having Zen time–Jenn time with my overwhelming thoughts. How can this be? I don't have time for this shit! Life sure had a funny way of flipping us off. But we still tried our best to find humor in it, because what else could we do?

We thoroughly enjoyed our time away, made it back home safely, and continued on with our schedules before my Ryan made me stop, take a deep breath, and pointed out, "Jenn, this is serious. You need to take this seriously." Now it makes sense to me why my coworker yelled out "Oh my God!" when I shared the diagnosis, while a few others teared up. This hideous, nasty diagnosis was a shock—total utter shock but then again, not really. After doing much research on it and comparing the years of my body woes, replaying past words from my doctors of unexplained tests results, and body issues, my coworker/work mom words came back to me as if it was yesterday, "You are the skinniest, health-conscious sick person I know." Oh my gosh, I was! I had vented for years to my mom, sister, Ryan, and friends, "I have all these old people issues—high cholesterol, hearing aids, bowel-and-bladder issues, polyps and cysts, partial hysterectomy," "I'm dizzy, can I just lay my head down," and "I swear I'm having constant ministrokes, all by my mid-thirties!" They were all the what-the-fucks of life, the fuckery of it all! How did I not see this coming?

We always knew something wasn't right with me. Stop giggling you over there. Be nice now! Something was going on with this body that was lent to me. (Uh, sir, I believe I got a lemon!) My good girl, pretty clean, gluten-free, and red meat–free diet seemed to help keep me settled for a bit until I needed to make yet another adjustment. I was constantly tweaking, detoxing, going vegan, experimenting with keto, doing plant-based protein shakes, and juicing. I was trying this and that all through the years. It was hard for everyone around me to keep up, "WTH [what the hell] is she doing now?" I was simply trying to find what agrees with this body. From time to time, my body would love me, then other times, it was in a full-out nasty, sharp, inflamed, and painful battle against me. But now we know. We know. You could give it a fancy technical book name claimed by several school years, earned titled, white-coat humans, but it's plain and simple to me. It's an *asshole* that has invaded my body, and it is not welcomed here! I do not want it; it feels like an alien, and I'm not liking it—not liking it one bit. Stomping my feet tossing around the middle finger, tears are flowing and throwing myself on the ground in a full tantrum, now passed out from exhaustion. Breathe, JennJenn, just breathe! Great, I need to step away because my freaking skin is prickling up now. For shit's sakes!

Then to add to the frustration of coming to terms of all the appointments, biopsies, blood work, prescriptions, and work-hour adjustments, we tried to keep up with social settings, we tried to keep up public appearances, client appointments, and playdates with friends with a kosher smile on. But one particular night out, I just couldn't do it anymore. I couldn't fake the smile or keep up with the conversation. I just wanted to lay down in a quiet, dark place and sleep away the meat-grinding pain, crawling, itching skin, weighed-down body, and nausea. I panicked, looked at Ryan, and choked out, "I don't feel well. I don't feel well at all." We got greeted with an annoyed, loud, bossy familiar female voice across the packed room, "Ryan, just take her home and come back!" Oh man, did Ryan and I make a "we are on the exact same page" eye beam glare to each other. I felt the steam boil up from my aching tummy, and the fire burning in my swollen throat as the dragon was about to unleash, #%&#@*#@!%*&@() (%#*@! In my mind, the obnoxious, hyper spider monkeys leaped across the multiple assortment of liquor and appetizers laid out on the kitchen island and spit a loogie in her contact eyeballs, smothered the guacamole dip through her sleek, hot-ironed hair, pinched her nasty-ass tongue, and added a layer of chocolate syrup to her foundation skin while I was shooting off my middle fingers like they were loaded machine guns! Whew, take a deep breath now, shake off that circus scene, and come back to reality. Instead, my concerned man gracefully, lovingly guided me to our truck and safely to our home *together*. We realized with that terribly, rude, hurtful moment we needed a break from other human beings until we could steady ourselves on this new path we were on. We get it now; some friends are just friends when you can continue to down plenty of alcohol together. Noted.

The constant doctor appointments were part of my new routine and resentfully worked into our monthly expenses. I was fully aware of the look on my doctor's and his nurse's faces when we started to backtrack some situations in my life, trying to figure out where the trigger was to bring this beast completely to the surface, screaming for attention. It seemed it was always in my life brought out at times but then back dormant for a season. But now it was daily, all day long. Then *boom*, we felt the culprit appeared.

At a yearly physical a few months prior, fall 2016, it was strongly suggested, due to The Zen Ranch adventure, to get a well, overdue tetanus shot—those kinds of shots I historically always turn down, but they caught me off guard in a very distracted moment, and I exhaustedly accepted. Before I knew it, all hell broke loose. I was in a middle of a medical shitshow! No other words for it—a total shitshow. Oh, it was messy, so disgustedly messy. Yes, there were several things through the years that pointed to this, but it all came to the surface immediately after that shot—fevers, hives, rashes, lumps and bumps, nausea, skin crawling, throat swelling, skin and nose sores, mouth vomits, and constant need for sleep—and here we are, now I'm the one that can't keep anything in me and running to the bathroom yelling for two-ply toilet paper. I could go on and on. It was such a shit-tastic time.

The doctors started in with a hundred questions of my medical paper trail, like my fainting in high school, but we blamed it on my teenage years and not taking care of myself; my extremely high cholesterol as a seventeen-year-old, how bizarre. They said it was like an overweight forty-year-old who smoked all their life, even though I was ideal weight and rarely ate red meat. Well, we said Mom and Dad have high cholesterol, so we blamed it on my family history. Way to go folks, thanks for sharing! In my twenties, I lost my hearing, but we pointed the finger at the birth of my boys, "JennJenn, you forgot to breathe!" In my late twenties and early thirties, I had bladder and bowel issues leading to surgeries and a partial hysterectomy, again pointing fingers that the birth of the kiddos did a grand number on my body. We'll just keep pointing fingers at the Timm bros—they did it; it's all their fault! My limbs would go numb, I would have moments of shortness of breath and poor concentration, so we put the blame on work stress. I started getting frequent piercing earaches that affected my skull to my cheeks to my jaw line and neck; the doctors said, "Your jaw must be out of alignment," even though the chiropractor didn't feel that was to blame. I was saying for years I felt I was having ministrokes; everyone laughed and said, "You are too busy as an overstressed working mom— you need to slow down." I couldn't sleep; the insomnia was bad. Again, we blamed on family history and a career in sales. I had unexplained rashes all over my body, fingers pointed at an allergy. Don't even get my started-on anger bursts. (I'm so sorry, everyone. I know now I just didn't feel well!) See the sideway jumping back and forth dance here? Pointing fingers here and there as work and family life was moving forward. So let's blame it on something and just keep busy trucking along and have another glass of wine!

Full distraction has always been our motto. We have things to do, places to be, responsibilities piling up, and we don't have time for whatever this nuisance is; just don't give it attention! I was a functioning person, but something wasn't quite right. The tetanus shot just woke it up to be brought out to the surface for all to see. It's show time, and the spotlight was on.

I have to say on a whole that I handled everything pretty darn well in the beginning. I took the lead from my folks in their own cancer journey and our Big-E in his celiac journey. I have to pat myself on the back because I kept a ton of it inside and struggled with the emotions, but then one day, I just found myself in an overwhelmed emotional roller coaster on the verge of exploding, and I had to scream at the top of my lungs. I think we all do this. We try to just go on with our daily lives and our own business like nothing is going on until something tilts us and we just can't take it anymore. The face staring back at me in the mirror those days had me pass, "It is what it is" pity party that usually only my moms and BFF-sister Jamie had to hear. Pass the shattered meltdowns only my Timm men would see. It had me totally and royally *pissed off.* The dragon was about to unleash, which was so not good for this vibrating, in-a-middle-of-a-war-against-itself body. I get lupus is a very scary and monstrous disease. It inflames and attacks different areas of my body all freaking day long. I get it could get worse and start attacking my organs. I get this is a life-threatening disease. I'm told these toxic medications are my new way of life. But seriously, the bloated, ashy face looking back in the mirror didn't look healthy to me at all. My dull, ghostly eyes didn't look alive. Nothing about it felt right—to be taking so many medications and still feel like dog shit. I was a drooling zombie sleeping my days away. It didn't sound right taking a medication to counteract the side effects of another. It concerned me that I was to have regular blood panels to check if the medications were affecting my liver and kidneys. Then eye panels to make sure the meds didn't do damage to my eyes. I was just utterly pissed how life had completely changed for me, but this lupus hadn't improved one bit and kept spiraling out of control. I would throw my tantrum but then shake it off with a few cuss words and tell myself, "I'm fine. It's fine. I'll go take the next round of meds followed by another nap. I'll stay out of the sun. I won't look at the damn wine [double ugh, goodbye, my friend] and take a deep breath while itching at my achy hives and rash-covered, bloated, and bruised up-from-the-meds body." Great, I need a drink of water now because I just mouth vomited. So it was appreciated when honest—too honest—niece Kals announced with perfect timing, "Aunt Jenn looks better fluffier."

> *My heartfelt, I'm-such-a-douche apology to our Ethan for saying the awful words: You're not getting special treatment; you have this disease. You need to learn to deal with this and get on with your day. Because if anyone said that to me while going through this health fiasco, I would have screamed, "Fuck off" and throat punched them. I am so terribly sorry, Big-E. I get it now. I so get it! Let's just sit on the floor together as you deserve a bear hug.*

The beginning of 2017 I was diagnosed with Sjogren's syndrome, lupus SLE, cutaneous lupus, and mixed connective tissue disease—whatever the hell that is. I was handed a handful of medications. I was told to avoid stress (uh huh), the sun, and a wide range of foods. The end of summer came fast, and we moved our Ethan off to college. Then the same month, I had a mammogram/ultrasound scare. Why not, let's keep hitting her while she's down. I passed out during the biopsy and ended up in the emergency room that evening. (My poor Ryan, we're still surprised he didn't have a nervous breakdown or heart attack. Thank goodness his parents were there for him). We were assured all would be just fine. I stepped down from my management position and scaled back my hours at work; I was told to take it easy. I followed every flipping instruction they gave me like the good girl I was. By the time December hit, I ended up in the emergency room again, followed up with a stomach emptying study, then diagnosed with gastroparesis. They put me on a liquid-purée diet and said it was most likely caused by the illness or the prescriptions. At this point, who cares. We crawled out of 2017 with a toss of a match burning that freaking bridge with a firm middle finger held high.

Confidently feeling great after entering the new year with a new natural and pure game plan in place, a true blessing from a concerned friend, but quickly the following week had me back in the doctor office and told it appears fibromyalgia has now joined this freaky party, a new prescription was suggested and ordered. I have to admit, I was defeated. Life can be so cruel. But then a blessing much needed Collins clan family weekend arrived. I'll be honest, I didn't want to go. I didn't want to be around happy humans. I didn't want to bring the party down. I was pissed the amazing life that I knew seemed over. But I sucked it up. I put on my big-girl panties heck even pants (well, soft leggings anyway) and showed up. Family, laughter and roller skating are the best prescription for *anything*! I so needed and enjoyed the weekend and returned home ready to take on the next month of appointments—an endoscopy, mammogram, and ultrasound follow-up, eye panel, and routine blood panels. I can roll with this. I got this. I am Collins strong—hear me roar! Family lifts us up, family has our back, family cheers us on, family reminds us who we are, and family keeps us going.

So yeah, we all have WTF moments and need a season to air out the cuss words a bit. Life throws us all kinds of nasty debris. Take a moment to sit back and take it all in then get a game plan in place. It's time to pack away the white flag, roll up the sleeves, attach a safety harness, get into a firm stance, and tackle that bitch head on. Distance yourself from anything that doesn't help join in on the battle; humans and environment may need to be eliminated. You just need to make a few tweaks to keep going. If you want it bad enough, you will get there, I promise. Whew, now wash your hands and mouth out with a pure, all-natural soap! We're still rolling on from here.

It's the Meds

Don't threaten me with the padded,
soundproof room. I have no
problems going there on my own!
—As seen on Pinterest

L ooking back to the beginning of this journey, it's hilarious that we made it through together. I shall take a bow now as I gave my men uncut entertainment—or as Ryan would say, "You certainly keep things interesting."

When hiccups in life happen, the wise folks will always say, "Before you know it, you will find a new normal." (Don't we all despise this phrase by now?) Well, if the things that were happening around me were the new normal for the Timm household, sweet baby Jesus, help us because this circus just got super freaking bizarre and awkward. Do we laugh, do we cry, do we throw a full-on tantrum, or do we just go to bed and sleep it all away? I took every one of those toxic prescriptions shoved my way. I read up on the diagnosis and joined some online support groups, which simply scared the crap out of me. I followed to the T what the "professionals" and seasoned lupis said to do. But holy fur baby land minds, did I become a walking, sometimes drooling, emotional zombie! My Ryan, my sackin' fish, just kissed me on my forehead and steered me to a couch, chair, or bed and took the reins like the boss that he is. I would try to get a sentence out and he would just laugh and confidently say, "It's the meds, dear," and I was out for the night.

One weekend morning, I had tried being vertical to attempt some household chores after double-digit hours of hard, wiped-out sleep but then must have quickly returned to bed in exhaustion only to be awoken soon after by a yelling, cussing, soaking wet teenage son appearing from the basement. Apparently, the alarm for the day was a kitchen sink waterfall on him. My attempt to be helpful around the house included me turning on the kitchen faucet, plugging the sink up, and leaning the mop next to the counter. Well, boys, the kitchen, floors, basement ceiling, and now one teenager are squeaky clean this fine early morning. You're welcome. Again, it's the meds! This was an "I'm so in the way ruining everything, the dogs are annoyed they are awake this early I'm making much more work for Ryan and now the teenager feels bad for yelling and upsetting his hot mess, train wreck, now-sobbing mama kind of morning during those "this is our new normal" days."

Toxic zombie I was, I would try to keep up my routine, only to find myself on a dog bed on the floor with no recollection of how I got there. Now, a few good years earlier, I would have pointed a finger at possibly a bottle or two of fabulous wine, but those days were long gone. Straight up H2O is my thirst quencher. I would roll over on a couch to find one of Ethan's groupies staring at me smiling, then off to dream land I returned. I'm sure I was all over social media as the past out mama. (Hand slap to the face.) I would find myself asleep in my vehicle outside work scaring the crap out of a coworker walking past my SUV on his way in for the day. Twenty minutes into work duties, I would need to lay down on that gifted couch in my office from the extremely understanding employer to appease this I-must-hibernate body.

As this bumpy path winded on, more A-holes (oops, that one snuck out from the last chapter) decided to join the unplanned, getting-out-of-control party. I couldn't remember my home address, so we blamed it on how similar it was to my work address. I couldn't remember my social security number, but we blamed it on how similar it was to, ha! I'm not saying it—thank you, nasty scammers, nice try! I couldn't remember my birthdate, but we laughed and said it was because I was twenty-seven for a good five years straight. Don't all us gals do that? I couldn't remember to shut off the water in the house on more than one occasion. In fact, I have flooded a few homes, but the blame went to I was trying to do way too much at once, the multi-tasking mama I was attempting to be. I couldn't remember where to pick people up; I couldn't remember words. I was going blank on what I did earlier in the day or even the day before, let alone the week before, or if I let the dogs back in the house after their potty breaks. I couldn't remember anything. I wanted to remember, and the more I would try, the more I wanted to put my head down because my head was spinning. I just froze up. We always had an excuse and laughed it off, but now we know, and now we have a name for it. It's Brain Fog, from the illness or the meds; we don't exactly know—it's just part of the party. Here I am still looking freaking adorable, but this party sucks!

To top off the fiasco that had become my life, I get a letter to report for what I thought was another standard lupus doctor's appointment at a new office. Ha, like there is any standards with this freaking disease. I was so confused when I showed up at this bland, from-the-eighties small office with only couches and the questions the dude with no white coat was asking me. See I didn't question it too much prior to the appointment because I was going to many appointments here, there, and everywhere. I was doing what I was told to do, and I was in a dazed and confused state because well, I am me. Then they slapped a heavy load of health terminology, testing, and toxic scripts on me. But after a few questions, I stopped in my tracks, looked around, squinted my eyes, and tilted my head, "Who are you again, and who referred me to you?" I'm almost embarrassed I'm sharing this and shake my head this didn't dawn on me sooner to deny the silly trip across town with my youngest son driving me, but it was a mandatory psych evaluation! On the instructed path, they had an antidepressant in my file, and I ditched it to the side, with many other prescriptions, after finding a much better, natural, and pure product for my system—a forever thank you, dear friends! I mean, the months of diagnosis after diagnosis and all the changes tossed at me like a hurricane, tsunami, and Iowa winter at once was rough, so terribly rough. So I'm sitting there on his smooth leather couch, heart racing and head spinning ready to burst in tears of embarrassment, or oh, dear, is the dragon about to be unleashed or possibly an outright insane laughter fit coming on, that "here I am, what the hell do I do?" Do I act JennJenn "normal" or fake it? Whose part do I play? What's going to get me out of this peculiar situation? Do I jump up and sprint for the door? Then again, my depth perception is completely off; therefore, most likely, I would smack my face right into the door. Do I get at least one call to a family member when they take me away in a strait jacket? Because I felt like this wasn't going to end with me walking out the door! Even to this day a few family members are wondering, "How on earth did she get out of there on her own?" I bet you are now too! It's okay, don't feel bad. I have always surprised the hell out of everyone.

Then get this, my hearing aids were once again well passed their expiration date and demanded to be replaced. So sure, let's keep adding to the pile of medical receipts, why not! Always doing the responsible adulting thing, we bit the bullet and confirmed the necessary testing, fitting, and purchase, which my techy Ryan was in full enthusiasm that this new modern set comes with the optional app that puts all notices, calls, and sounds from my cell phone directly into my ears. In true Ryan style, he set up this feature while I was snoozing away, and he forgot to tell me or he told me while I was not listening. Okay, fine, I'm sure I simply forgot, but I so got the message while sitting in a meeting the next day when there was ringing followed with talking in my head! As I ask out to the group, "Do you hear that?" matched with "What the hell is wrong with you?" stares. I admit, I get those often. Here I thought I was going loco dealing with everything, the mind game of it all, coming to terms with what my body was doing, and now I literally had voices in my head—commit me now! I'll take that straitjacket now! JennJenn has had it. Someone raise the white flag for me; I'm too drained.

Delicate ears, be ready on this one! While out for a drive, as we often do, Ryan took a turn into an area lined with shops. I yelled out, "Oh look at those fabulous fuckers!" Pause, whoa. We awkwardly looked at each other and laughed a little. I sheepishly admitted, "I'm not sure where that came from, but I meant spinners, fabulous spinners." Well, isn't this "fun" now, the copycat to Tourette's, weird words were inserted here and there appeared often during those it's-the-meds days. And that, folks, officially confirmed I had to start the process of leaving the workforce. No more reduced hours—I need to be home. We all decided, maybe JennJenn shouldn't be in public anymore and needed more Zen time–Jenn time at home so my head and body could rest, fully rest. Pat myself on the back, I finally understood and, this time, didn't put up a fight. Yes, I may have stretched this out a year too long, but the day had come. I just couldn't do it anymore. I certainly gave it a good run.

It got to a point where it was a vicious, expensive cycle of running to the doctor's office and taking prescriptions, which included harsh steroids in order to just show up at work half a day. I attempted this song and dance for over a year when it was time, finally time, to throw in the towel. My dad's question woke me up, "Jenn, what are you doing?" and our wise Evan's sweet words rang in my ears from many years ago when we were out and about in our social crowd, "Go home. I want to go home. It's time to go home." So I took the hint and now am no longer a part of the sad statistic that I was so determined to be in the 31 percent club: the percentage of lupus adults who are able to work full-time.

> *December 2018, I walked through the doors of my career as an employee for the last time. I'm not good at goodbyes, but it wasn't a goodbye—it's a "see you later," as some wonderful friendships were made there.*
> *Now on to Zen time–Jenn time for good!*

I'm hard of hearing, socially awkward, have no problem saying what I think and feel, full of meds, and those chipmunk cheeks you just want to squeeze, but watch out, I'm steroid-hangry and may bite your head off! I'll get through this; it's just quite the mental game when my coping skills for years and years has been keeping very busy, distracted, and having the wine take me away.

The world may feel like it's falling apart. Doors may be closing. You may feel like you are being stripped of everything you worked your buns off for and built. But this is doable. You can do this. It's going to be okay. Now chin up, take a deep breath, wipe away those tears, even the nose snot. You got this. You have plans for yourself, may be new plans, but there are always other plans to tackle—yell back at life, "This isn't me! It's the meds!"

The Angels that Get Us Through

Life isn't about waiting for
the storm to pass... It's about
learning to dance in the rain.
—Vivian Greene

Now I could go on and on about my Ryan, my sackin' fish—a tea-making, back-rubbing, steam-mopping, chick-flick-getting man. A whole mushy novel, but we'll just get a room instead, and I'll shine the spotlight onto the other angels in my life.

Ryan came from good folks. They certainly stepped in and helped out whenever and wherever they could without ever making it feel like a burden. We so appreciated it, and I can't thank them enough for taking some of the stress off Ryan, knowing he had someone to lean on too. The spouse struggles with their own fears watching life as they know it shift. My in-laws are the best.

I remember many years ago after a few months of back-to-back surgeries and much time in bed recuperating my saint of a mother came to stay with us to help Ryan, while he was keeping control of his busy work responsibilities and our early teen boys' color-coded calendar of activities. She spoiled me with the most adorable loungewear to heal in the weeks to come. I was all tucked in under my white feather down as my beautiful, blessed beast and pal at the time, Ed, our beloved 120-pound boxer, was at my feet while I slept. He guarded me and the door like it was his mission to protect his human at all costs. How dare anyone or anything ever hurt her again. He took this duty seriously and would even stand firmly over me anytime my mom tried to enter the bedroom to check on me. They came to a truce when he allowed her to bring in a rocking chair at the end of the bed for her to sit and read near me while sipping on her tea. He stayed guarded with one eye on her at all times. We chuckle about it now, but it was a bit intimidating for her as she just wanted to lie with me, hold me, and carry the concern, but he stole that duty or time from her. As a loving mother, she kept trying, and he wouldn't budge from his duties.

> *A dog doesn't care if you are rich or poor,*
> *educated or illiterate, clever or dull. Give*
> *him your heart and he will give you his.*
> —John Grogan

Let's get this straight: they are not just dogs. It dawned on me one lazy Sunday morning at the age of forty-three why on earth my Ryan has allowed me to have multiple fur babies at once. He knew fur babies are my squad, and I prefer the company of these furry creatures over humans any day. I can't explain it; I just do better around them. My arms ache for them. And I may be a bit known in the family to spoil, pay attention to, and photograph these fur babies more often than the human boys. They may quite possibly have many more toys than my Timm boys ever had and have a spot in our bed when the human babies were *never* allowed. Yes, we all know Ryan rarely says no to me and would do anything to make me happy because he is head over heels in love with me or completely scared shitless of me, whatever you want to call it, but truly he allowed many at a time because I um, well, I am *needy*. Yep, me, totally needy. I needed hugs. I needed attention. I wanted to be snuggled and kissed often. I wanted to have eyes that stared deep into my soul and confirmed that I was adored, loved, and understood. I wanted a body to hold and dance with when a good song came on. And well, after twenty-three years of marriage, he needed to recruit backup in this area. These little fellas were the same way, and we had the love, time, and resources to share with them. Bundles of love piled on my lap about 90 percent of the time, while a few more were nearby eyeing me. My little balls of snugglers and Ryan was free to sit chill as can be next to me with his remote in his hand, always available to offer up a smile, wink, and a free hand for me to hold. The same little fellas who were always on my lap were my own personal little furnaces in bed too. Their peaceful snoring would put me right to sleep and drowned out Ryan's snoring that would normally annoy the hell out of me. This, folks, is relationship goals—a happy situation for all parties. Freed up Ryan's time, energy, and quite possibly a pillow smothered over him in the dead of the night, kidding (or am I?). Dogs understand us. They sense when we are hurting, not feeling well and just need some comfort. My man was at ease away at his office knowing I was taken care of and not alone or lonely at home with our grumble. We healed together; fur babies are the best prescription for any ailment or nightmare you may find yourself in. Again, adopt—don't shop!

> *If you mess with the big sister, then there*
> *is always a younger, crazier sister behind*
> *her that you don't want to mess with!*
> —As seen on Pinterest

This is true. This is my baby sister Jamie. Our love story shall continue to grow as we have each other to lean on daily throughout this freaky journey. I am so blessed with my sackin' fish Ryan, the Timm boys, the fur baby snugglers, two sets of parents checking in on me often, friends' texts, amazing coworkers at the time, but of course, my sister, who always knows how to add humor to my days, would take the lead. Everyone needs a Jamie in their lives, with her out-of-the-blue "keep fucking going" gifts and text messages of, "I had a dream about you last night. We were at the bar having a drink and talking, when this guy sat down and was just being a jerk to you. Complete jerk. His name was Lupus! Yep, I lost it and kicked his ass right there!"

That younger sister of mine cracks me up. No matter the situation, she makes any bad, ugly cry day disappear with a text. Giggling teary grin on. My sister is a freaking kickass, crazy rock!

My long-time employer, who I could say was a true friend through the years, helped tremendously on this bumpy, storming road. He tried everything possible to take some stress off me during this time of coming to terms with this freakshow. He added a couch to my office so I could rest whenever I needed to. He allowed reduced hours in the office because this body was screaming, "I'm weak, exhausted, vibrating, and hurting! Calm it down, now!" On the surface, most would see a hard, stern, intimidating man, but to the core, he was understanding and caring. He made this journey so much better, and I will be forever grateful for him. Even my medical team were impressed and wished more of their patients had an employer like him to help them through their own transition with these nasty diagnoses. It is a mental game losing the battle of our body, mind, friendships and, most of us, our careers that we worked our asses off to achieve—losing the life as we knew it. I can't thank him enough for helping ease into the transition.

My incredible dear friend Danielle made days simply beautiful by checking in on me. Diagnosis and illnesses change people, and it's the new angels that appear in our lives that save the day and help us through, but then as quick as she came, she was taken away. One morning, I found myself stunned and wrestling with emotions when learning my dear friend had suddenly passed away. I only physically met her and Papa Scott once when handing over our Lenny Benny Roo to her, a rescue puggle we fostered for a handful of months. I knew from her application that she was someone special and the one to trust with this lone wolf. From day one she knew how hard it was on me; therefore, she included me on all day-to-day duties, photos, and his growing stylish wardrobe. She made sure he had a jacket for every occasion. I never met her husband, Steve, or her brother Adam, but she made sure I knew them as if I was part of the family.

A Wisconsin gal and an Iowa gal, a Packers fan and a Vikings fan, a blonde and a brunette, a social chick and a homebody, but we had so much in common with our frequent conversations; I cherished our bond. We shared the same odd humor of talking dog talk for hours with "Hey, Carol!" references that we were just sure our fur babies were saying to us. We never got to share a drink together, but we would have lengthy conversations on building our dream Bloody Mary. I knew about her health struggles and fears and she knew of mine. When my Ethan brought home a Wisconsin gal from college, she offered to do a drive-by to the neighboring town to see what kind of people they were. Her texts always started with "Hey, Doll," which made me feel special, not forgotten, and alive again—a simple, "Hey Doll." Just the day before the terrible news was announced, we were sharing numerous mesmerizing food videos we were never ever going to cook. We encouraged each other and leaned on each other through technology. My heart broke in two for everyone hurting in Wisconsin that she physically touched, as an angel had left us all. RIP, my dear sweet friend. You are so adored and are terribly missed—I love you, doll!

My Timm boys—oh, those deep-dimple-smiling Timm boys. Our weeks needed an eye-glittering Ethan.

His humor and energy are a great start to the week and a pump up to the weekend. Ethan brought deep belly laughs, tears down the face, jaw hurting, and stomach aching from laughing so hard, as he replays his days. He distracts us from all our headaches and fears of the moment. If there was silence around our E, it was because we couldn't catch our breaths from laughing and shaking our heads from his stories. Ethan is the backyard party, shooting fireworks off in the sky. Then there is our dreamy, eccentric Evan—the "front porch rocking chair taking in the midnight stars and hearing the crickets" chill Evan. Every day needs an Evan. Evan brings a calmness to the storm of life. If there was silence around Evan, it was from his peaceful vibe, pondering with a gentle smile what he had just said, reminiscing and visualizing his calm observation. He brings a warm heart and a genuine smile. His quick, dry wit and laid back, deep voice stories bring campfire soothing to the day and is oh so welcomed. The big guy above certainly knew what he was doing placing these Timm men in my life. I am beyond spoiled and blessed.

Look around you, those angels are in your life. They may not be the people in your circle the longest, nor are they always the blood related or even human, but they are there. They are the ones you feel most warm and fuzzy near. They are the ones asking how you are, cheering you on, and calling you sweet names that make you smile and feel special. They are the ones that can turn you from ugly crying to snort laughing. They appear when you least expect it. You better make sure you pay attention, welcome it, and hang tight to those angels to get you through your darkest days.

Messed with the Wrong Freaking Gal

The greatest, most rewarding adventure
emerged during our darkest nightmare
—Toxic Zombie to Hemp Alive
—#JennHempAlive

It's true, I never wanted to leave the workforce. I loved working; it was always my escape. At first, I felt like it was so unfair and cruel. I crawled and fought my way to the top in a male-dominant industry. Now here I am homebound. I often found myself prisoner inside our own home at The Zen Ranch staring out the large picture glass window at the beautiful large backyard we designed, the paradise that we had created together as a family. It was always there waiting for me, staring back at me, and taunting me, because I couldn't get out during the sunny days to play due to the harsh restrictions put upon me and my body saying, "Heck no, don't you dare do it, JennJenn!" It started to really wear me down, and I couldn't get away from the view because it was me who put these large windows everywhere in the home to bring the outdoors in.

I would patiently—well, not so patiently because I am a Collins and an Annear—so I would just sit there waiting for the sun to go down to venture out like a vampire; but then by the time the outdoor dimmer gave me the green light, I was too exhausted from the day to partake in the outdoor festivities, so I'd push that feeling aside and try again the next day. It was all I could do.

Just breathe, everything is
going to be o-k-a-y.
—Evan Dennis

I was trying to adapt to my new instructions, finding my way with the existence of these monsters within, doing what I was told because that is what we are supposed to do. Be a good girl and do what the dude with the fancy paid-for-with-a-mounding-debt-earned title tells you to do. But the whole thing didn't feel right to me. This can't be how the journey will be now. I started crawling my way through books, talking with friends, combing the internet, and questioning this path. My pretty awesome lupus doctor has a way with words; knowing the fire in me, he gently planted in my mind how this new journey should go. He actually said to me—and it was my awakening—moment that this is my journey, my way, "You make an awful patient, [pause] which is good. You'll get this figured out on your own and not fall victim to this horrible disease like so many do."

I sat moping in my chair day in and day out of what was stripped from me after all my years of hard work. I felt the universe kept tagging me, shoving me, and tripping me, until one day I snapped, and the dragon fought through and screamed, *"Oh hell no!* I am not this person. I will *not* be this person!" I jumped up and physically shook off *that* person—the mopey person, the "victim." I absolutely refused to be *that* person, as I have plans for myself. Get out of my damn way! *Badass* panties are on. Crown is straightened; I remembered who my family is—Collins strong we are. High boots on and ready to kick some ass, I grabbed Mr. Lupus and his nasty cousins by the throat, firmly stating, "You messed with the wrong freaking gal. You were never invited on this adventure, so you better follow my road rules!"

Along this journey, I found out an awful lot had to go wrong for me to end up in the right place. "Things happen for a reason"—I hated when people said that to me. I used to think our speed bumps along the ride were a punishment, but in all honestly, they are a true blessing for a new fabulous view, and our family has never been closer! We just need to look at the situation in a new light. Doctors and family members telling me to "knock it off and slow down, damnit," gave me a chance to stay home, take a deep breath, and rethink things. I was burned out at a roller-coaster sales career, ready for a change. Had these diseases not jumped on board, I would have stayed put and settled in for the long haul, missing out on many other fabulous opportunities. Had I not left the workforce, I would not have become this committed, loud, and proud CBD advocate that I am—halleluiah! Did that make a huge difference, gaining all these amazing, supportive friendships and helping so many others. My first published book, *It's Been One Hell of a Ride*, would still be sitting idle on the side of the road. And this book you are enjoying right now (or possibly dropping your jaw over) would just be jumbled words in my foggy brain. Ethan's celiac taught us very early to watch what we are eating. Because we were so busy given our hectic schedules and fast-paced lifestyle, we would have been that nasty, easy-peasy fast-food family. Thankfully, we couldn't be. For years, I wanted to quit drinking. *Bam!* Give me a scary disease or five, so I'm forced to stop with no more excuses. Well, not stop 100 percent, but at least 99.8 percent. I mean really, come on.

So it's true; I accept it now, everything does happen for a reason. See the humor, blessings and lessons in your journey. These diseases steered us on the right path to pay better attention to what is going into our bodies, what our bodies are telling us. It opened our eyes to what is going on in our society with our food source. If you can't pronounce or recognize the word in the ingredients, you probably shouldn't be ingesting it. It made us rethink running to the doctor's office and taking every little thing they give us, instead of making much-needed lifestyle changes. The big guy up above put plants on this earth for a reason.

I was mourning a gal—I once was—but I realized I was becoming a gal to be pretty darn proud of and happy to be! I have this constant love-hate relationship battle with my body. It's a confirmed and documented five-time A—hole that tries to attack itself every single hour of every day. I want to exchange it. It's exhausting, it's frustrating, and it's depressing, but I refuse to give in. I could go on and on about this A—hole who invaded my body and brought along his cousins, but I don't want to concentrate on that. I'm not giving it any more attention than necessary. I've got plans for myself, so here is what we are going to do: we're going to make some major adjustments and continue with my plans. I remind myself often that it could always be worse, so I'll deal and change my thoughts from "why me" to "it is what it is, so let's find a way to make this work and keep rolling." I just sarcastically and adorably smirk, raise that middle finger, say a cuss word under my breath, and give this hot mess of a body some love with plant-based superfoods, comfy attire sprinkled with the fella's fur glitter, add some dazzlingly earrings and a touch of mascara. Now let's get this glorious day started—because I'm still here!

Heck, look at me. I don't have to even wear pants most days; PJs are my daytime attire. I get regular massages and can take naps whenever I want with the pug fellas. Best of all, I don't have to leave home or be around humans if I just don't feel like it. And the good days, I'm going to get my buns up and make the most of the day doing everything I can. I may have to ask for help and things may take a bit more time than before, but we're just going to do this dance back and forth until I accomplish that list, that vision board, those dreams I see so vividly. So who's winning now? Just see the good in every situation. It's there; it's always, always there!

Now you see how it hasn't been easy living with our Ethan and definitely not me for that matter. No fault of our own—this is life. The big guy above knew exactly what he was doing pairing Ethan and I with calm, laid back Ryan and Evan. We are all dealt different cards in the game. Yet we didn't completely concentrate on the hiccups. We didn't focus on the woes too long. We hopped, skipped, and jumped over the potholes in this journey. We hurdled over obstacles with ease and a few times circled back and filled in those potholes for good. It wasn't an easy one although certainly could have been far worse on this journey. We have plans for ourselves, and we found a way to make things happen. It's true, the greatest, most rewarding adventure emerged during our darkest nightmare, and we didn't give up on our happily ever after. We won't give up—what a ride, what an adventure, what a journey!

It's okay to sit back and reevaluate what doesn't feel right, to question what doesn't seem right, and to overhaul your lifestyle when it isn't working right. It's up to you—no one else but *you*—to find a way to feel better, look better, and be better! Remove the gluten from your life, take a few naps, and add in a good, pure, high-quality CBD oil (I personally know an adorable gal to help you with that). Today's the day to take care of *you*. Feel alive again. Make the changes necessary to be alive again; don't make do. Don't give in. Don't you dare raise that white flag, baby!

Well, we did it! We got to live our dream out and create a paradise space to play, chill, and be wild and free, a space to completely enjoy with our Timm boys in their last years at home with us. It may not have turned out to be for the long haul as we once envisioned in the beginning of the adventure. It simply turned out to be extra work we just weren't game to keep up with the new journey we were on, and that's okay. All hands in together—we did an amazing job, and boy, did we have some epic moments! Ryan and I were thrilled to move on to the next phase in our lives. The view of peace and quiet in our brand-spankin'-new Zen Ranch II, the ultimate chill pad. The only emotion we were feeling was giddiness—no map, no guide, no problems! Plus, no yardwork or snow removal in Iowa either—total chill pad. I can't wait to see what the road ahead brings. Watch us with our big nets going after those dreams. Here we go! Let's keep this adventure rolling!

About the Author

J ennifer Collins-Timm published her first book, *It's Been One Hell of a Ride*, while enjoying Zen time—Jenn time at her home, with her husband, Ryan. As her two Timm boys are out on their own adventures as young adults, she is a proud stay-at-home dog mom to her three elder pug-fellas. She spends her days planning road trips with her man on her arms,  enlightening others on the remarkable benefits of a pure, high-quality CBD oil*, and considering more books.

Jennifer writes her stories based off her unconventional yet resourceful and productive way of handling motherhood and life in general with sarcasm and laugh-out-loud moments. Plus, her Timm men and fur babies continue to give her great material to work with!

JennHempAlive@gmail.com